A COOKBOOK
by the Junior League of Minneapolis

Junior League of Minneapolis
Minneapolis, Minnesota
1987

The Junior League of Minneapolis is an organization of women committed to promoting voluntarism and improving the community through the effective action and leadership of trained volunteers. Its purpose is exclusively educational and charitable.

The Junior League of Minneapolis reaches out to women of all races, religions, and national origins who demonstrate an interest in and commitment to voluntarism.

Proceeds from CELEBRATED SEASONS are used to support community projects and services of the Junior League of Minneapolis. Some of those projects include: Success by 6 Partners Project; 1991 International Summer Special Olympics; Project Break-Through; Violence Against Women Conference; 3 R's - Reduce, Recycle, Reuse; Cancer Awareness Research and Education (C.A.R.E.); Women in Leadership; Minnesota Teen Pregnancy Prevention; Project Giving/Presents of Life; Teen Outreach Program; and Too Early Pregnancy.

©JLM Publishing, 1987
©Elizabeth Hood Anderson, 1987
1st Printing, 1987, 20,000 copies
2nd Printing, 1990, 10,000 copies
ISBN 0-9618235-0-X

PRINTER:
S. C. Toof & Company, Memphis, Tn.

RECIPE EDITOR:
Betsy Norum

CONTENT DESIGN:
Morgan Williams and Associates
Minneapolis, Minnesota

ARTWORK:
Elizabeth Hood Anderson
Bloomington, Minnesota

COVER DESIGN:
Graphic Design
Erica Goldfarb

CREATIVE PORTIONS OF MANUSCRIPT:
Amy Campbell Lamphere

Photography
John Danicic, Jr.

WINE INFORMATION:
John Farrell
Haskell's International Wine Room
Minneapolis, Minnesota

Food Stylist
Barbara Strand

Additional copies of CELEBRATED SEASONS may be obtained by writing:

CELEBRATED SEASONS
JLM Publishing
428 Oak Grove
Minneapolis, Minnesota 55403
(612) 871-8423

Please enclose your return address with a check payable to JLM Publishing in the amount of $18.95 per book plus $2.50 postage and handling per book. (Price subject to change without notice) Minnesota residents, add sales tax of $1.23 per book.

Please send any inquiries regarding the purchase of the limited edition prints of color artwork in this book to the same address listed above.

Cover Photo: Harvest Cheesecake pictured, recipe on page 188

Table of Contents

Menus and Party Plans

Recipes

- Poultry
- Seafood
- Lamb/Pork
- Beef/Veal

The Cookbook Committee

Special thanks to the following Junior League of Minneapolis members who have worked on this committee and have contributed to the success of this fundraiser.

Betsy Allen
Debbie Austin
Cammy Baer
Barb Beard
Mary Bergaas
Leslie Berkshire
Ann Besinger
Susan Bisanz
Jennifer Bixler
Geraldine Bloomer
Bonnie Bohn
Terry Bolin
Judy Bradford
Julie Brennan
Toni Cady
Marcia Carlson
Cheryle Clausman
Nancy Clemens*
Mary Ann Clifford
Desiree Collings
Kris Cosgrove
Page Cowles
Carol Cronk*
Bette DeMars
Jerri DeVard
Maggie Dickhaus
Karen Divine
Julie Halverson Drake
Judy Ebrahim
Ginger Elverud
Margaret Everist
Joanie Fitzgibbons
Betsy Foster

Kathy Fox
Kay Franzen
Susan Garity
Valeria Golden
Sue Gullickson
Julia Hallquist
Pamela Hamel
Carol Hancock
Barb Hendricks*
Karen Himle
Liz Hopwood
Bev Hyatt
Jane Johnson
Sue Jorgensen
Terrie Jorgensen
Nancy Jurkovich
Stefanie Karon
Kate Keilty
Nancy Kloehn
Pam Korell
Coralyn Koschinska
Mary Kuhn
Mary Kunz
Amy Campbell Lamphere
Nancy Lindahl
Terese Lynch
Barbi Mahoney
Deborah Margeson
Sharon Mattison*
Nancy McCarthy
Julie McGarvey
Nancy McGoldrick
Ellie Meade

Kristine Melloh
Barb Melsen
Judy Mendesh
Patty Merker
Sara Messelt
Jane Nilsen
Betsy Nimmo
Ellie Noyes
Andy Otness
Mary Kay Pilla
Stella Rezac
Mary Robinson*
Helen Rockwell
Karla Rockwell
Mimi Ryerse
Lisa Schaller
Nancy Schnoebelen
Pat Sinclair*
Linda Skarphol
Julie Stout
Kris Strawbridge
Kathy Suddendorf
Mary Taylor
K. K. Tesar
Nancy Thysell-Johnson
Debbie Tranter
Carol Waldron
Julie Wannamaker
Sally Warner
Barbara Weikart
Dode Wheaton
Mary Lange Zbikowski

* Chaired Committee

"CELEBRATED SEASONS, A Cookbook by the Junior League of Minneapolis" began back in 1985 as a fundraiser of the Minneapolis Junior League. It was an exciting venture, involving many League volunteers, utilizing their professional skills in marketing, production, sales and distribution, and, quite naturally, cooking and entertaining.

The original committee grew to over 50 members — and extended much, much further, tapping the talents of the general membership and the community, who supported this project by submitting and testing recipes, and suggesting form and content.

In truth, the project began many years before this, in family kitchens, over grandmothers' and great aunts' stoves. These gatherings were simple affairs, centered around tables brimming with the best those early kitchens could offer. They celebrated the wild fruits and flowers of our woods and riverbanks, the game from our forests, the fish from our numerous lakes.

The early Minnesotans celebrated traditional holidays and, in keeping with their pioneering zeal, invented new ones of their own. Cooking traditions mingled too, and new flavors were explored — a culinary tradition was developed that was uniquely their own.

Recently, new technology, the world of business, and a growing community of artists have discovered this rich region. Minnesota is being settled by those with palates and expectations that have raised her cooks' senses to new levels of flavorful possibilities. It is a continuous learning process, expanding repertoires and the skills to support them, creating new seasons to celebrate and developing new friendships to share them.

It is the League's hope that, with this book, you will be encouraged to discover your own celebrations, while you enjoy the seasons that have made our city so special.

"CELEBRATED SEASONS," A Cookbook by the Junior League of Minneapolis, is an entertaining tour of the city we know best. Hosts and hostesses from all over Minneapolis have shared special recipes, gracious and uncomplicated menus, and original finishing touches, creating the book to turn to for advice on planning any celebration.

The change of seasons, so beautiful in our northern city, also signals a change of tastes, the discovery of new, fresh flavors, special reasons for revelry and happy events to celebrate. CELEBRATED SEASONS offers over 250 recipes and suggestions for making every meal a memorable one.

This creative collection has been carefully selected to present the best of Minneapolis, and, Minnesota—delicious and different recipes, imaginative menus, and a unique planning matrix for personalizing any party with infinite flavor combinations. Colored by the beautiful scenes that have inspired our demanding cooks and contributors, CELEBRATED SEASONS is a treasure for book-lovers and gourmets alike, and a welcome addition to any kitchen.

Spring Parties

Green Thumb Luncheon

A Ladies Lunch for Eight to Ten

Season Opener

A Patio Opening Party for Eight to Ten

Bridle Party

A Hunt Supper for Eight to Ten

Passages

A Turning Point Birthday Party for Twenty to Thirty

Minnehaha Falls

Green Thumb Luncheon
A Ladies Lunch for Eight to Ten

*White Sangria with Fresh Fruit

*Steering Committee Luncheon Shrimp Salad

Steamed Fresh Asparagus with Browned Butter

*Rafferty's Golden Cheese Popovers

*Lemon Creme Dessert

No sooner than the flow of Christmas catalogs slows, Minneapolis mailboxes become filled with colorful missives from the flower companies. This intrusion sets would-be gardeners dreaming about long, sunny afternoons spent working in neatly cultivated grounds, spilling with flowers and the freshest vegetables — perfect for brightening the home and heaping full the salad bowl.

Celebrate this season of new beginnings by gathering a group of your favorite fellow gardeners for lunch — maybe in the sunroom or on the patio? Here is a time to dream big and plan the ultimate garden, while you are surrounded by supportive friends who might be coaxed into helping those dreams come true!

Staple and "bow" a package of seeds to colorful notecards for the invitation, being sure to include all the pertinent party information. If you're fortunate enough to have a yardful of early blooms, you can tie a bouquet with a pretty ribbon, attach a simple invitation card, and hand deliver to neighborhood friends.

If weather permits, serve the first drinks on the patio so everyone can soak in the fresh air and sun. Big straw hats are perfect decorations here — fill them with flowers or pass them around to wear!

Greet guests with a punch glass full of fruity sangria, made even more festive by floating some blooms in the bowl. Decorate your party room with clay pots full of flowers and clever arrangements of "edible art" — vegetable centerpieces constructed of baby carrots, zucchini, eggplants and peppers, julienned sticks of celery, freshly cleaned and peeled mushroom caps and radishes, and a handful of cherry tomatoes.

Set cored, leafy red and green cabbages filled with your favorite dipping sauce in the middle of the abundantly piled vegetables — supplemented with mounds of seeded crackers and tortilla chips — and encourage nibbling while the guests gather.

Set the luncheon table with as many mixed and matched patterns of flowered china that you can afford (or borrow!). Beautiful, many-layered tablecloths can be simply

*Recipe included in book

stitched from inexpensive cotton calicos, or layer pretty, patterned sheets. Tuck your best silver in "flowers" of folded cloth napkins and have personalized cotton garden gloves, or packages of seeds, marking each guest's place.

Toss the main course salad in the biggest wooden bowl you can muster. Baskets of Cheese Popovers are ready to pass around the table and that sure sign of spring — fresh asparagus — is served, steaming hot, with a light drizzle of browned butter.

Lemons appear for dessert, as Creme-stuffed shells, frozen until ready to serve with coffee and tiny tea cookies. Garnish the plates with flowers, a final flourish to the first party of Spring.

<u>A WINE SUGGESTION:</u> French White Burgundy or Napa Chardonnay.

Season Opener
A Patio Opening Party for Eight to Ten

Beer and Wine

*Green Gazpacho

*Artichoke Hearts with Fresh Mint

*Whole Grilled Salmon with Dill Sauce

*Apricot and Avocado Rice

Sourdough Rolls

*Amaretto Creams with Fresh Fruit

Springtime is an important season for Minneapolitans who have been known to sometimes spend from October to April blanketed in white. There are many festive openings at this time, some involving sports, others involving theatre productions and art galleries. The opening described here is dedicated to the advent of the grilling season — and the season's first barbecue.

Your invitation should be the first signal — try tying a checkered picnic bow around an inexpensive grilling fork and attaching a card with the party information. Plan a weekend afternoon to deliver the details of the cookout, and to reconnect with friends who've been hibernating all winter!

Sweep off the patio and wipe down the grill — be sure to have plenty of charcoal, lighter fluid, matches and marshmallows on hand. Plan the party for early in the evening so you can take advantage of the spectacular spring sunset while enjoying cocktails on the patio. Chill a galvanized tub of fancy beers, favorite wine and flavored sparkling mineral water.

Drape the scene with banners, flags or bunting for the event, or settle for some twinkle lights in the tree and several new pots of flowering plants. Set a picnic-style table in the formal dining room; (it will probably still be too cool to spend the whole evening outdoors), the unexpected mix of styles will add to the evening's fun.

Pass mugs of Green Gazpacho to sip on the patio while the grill is heating up. A buffet sideboard inside will hold the bowls of artichoke salad and fruited rice, but make sure everyone has a chance to see the whole salmon in its glistening grilled splendor before the skin is removed and the rich portions are passed around. Pass around a bowl of the green

*Recipe included in book

dill sauce, a beautiful accompaniment. A basket of chewy sourdough rolls could fill out the pretty menu.

The dessert, too, is a special treat. Amaretto Creams are liqueur-tinged frozen creams, spilling with the freshest berries the market will bear. Enjoy the confections with strong cups of coffee as the opening festivities draw to a close. Soon there will be other season opening celebrations; cheering on the ballteam or sitting around the campfire telling stories about "the one that got away" . . . and the one that looked so impressive hot off the grill tonight.

<u>A WINE SUGGESTION:</u> French White Burgundy or Napa Chardonnay

Bridle Party
A Hunt Supper for Eight to Ten

*Bootlegs

*Bleu Cheese-Stuffed Shrimp

*Butterflied Leg of Lamb with Minted Hollandaise

*Rice with Raisins and Pine Nuts

*Zucchini and Red Pepper Saute

*White Chocolate-Raspberry Tart

One of Minneapolis' newest entertainment treasures is the thoroughbred race track to the south of the city, Canterbury Downs. Hostesses have taken to celebrating the introduction to this sport of kings in a manner that ranges from spontaneous infield picnics to Winner's Circle formal balls. This Bridle Party falls somewhere in the middle of these, a clubby hunt supper to share with friends, after a successful afternoon at the track, or to celebrate the coming of Spring and the running of the Kentucky Derby.

Send an invitation that sets the tone for the evening's events — either a racing form that describes the party as an odds-on favorite for fun, or a "jockey club" notecard that tells of your plans. Tell guests to dress in their best jodhpurs and hunt jackets, or Ascot-right finery, or simply in their favorite comfortable tweeds and colorful shetlands.

Deck your tables with jockey-silk colors and put together a large flowery horseshoe to greet the guests at the door. This horseshoe motif can be repeated on a smaller scale in your centerpiece, maybe a part of a "racy" assemblage of jockey helmet, riding whip, a jockey's silk scarf, racing forms and win tickets that "just didn't come in!" Every table is prettier by candlelight, and be sure to put on music to suit the party mood.

The drink of the day is Bootlegs, a minty Julep-like cooler that will be sure to elevate the attitude of even the day's biggest track loser. With these potent potables, pass a platterful of Bleu Cheese-Stuffed Shrimp, tangy crustaceans that can be spread ahead and chilled until serving time.

Napkin wrap the silverware and tie with bright silk ribbon. "Plate" the supper in the kitchen and serve your guests with all the aplomb of one who is manor born. Be sure to pass extra Hollandaise to pour over the rich lamb — its minted aroma will be sure to have the diners calling for more. Pilaf-like Rice with Raisins and Pine Nuts makes a savory accompaniment, and a saute of red peppers and zucchini adds colorful accent.

*Recipe included in book

Dessert is a winning White Chocolate and Raspberry Tart cut into wedges and served with plenty of fresh coffee. Settle into the evening recalling the day's events, lucky choices, sure-bet techniques, and the beauty of a spring afternoon at the races.

A WINE SUGGESTION: St. Emilion or California Merlot

Passages
A Turning Point Birthday Party for Twenty to Thirty

*Champagne Punch   *Grand Sparkling Punch

*Fresh Mushroom Paté

*Asparagus in Mini-Crepes

*Hot Mustard Sauce with Crudites

*Avocado Supreme

*Feta Shrimp Triangles

*Sausage Puffs

*Crispy Chicken Wings with Sesame

*Very Intense Brownies

*Merry Cheesecake Bars

Birthday Cake

Fresh Fruit

While some will argue that every birthday is a special occasion, there are certain birthdays that deserve to be celebrated above and beyond the simple cake, card, and candles theme. Turning point birthdays in particular — those extra-big days when the numbers come up ending with resolute "0's" — require careful planning, tactful realization . . . and often many surprises!

Whether you decide to surprise your guest of honor or not, one thing is for certain — the party should be perfectly planned to delight and dazzle the celebrant. Surround him or her with all their favorite things: music, food, decor and people! And don't forget to bring cameras and plenty of film! (Even better, videotape the events!)

This party has been planned as an evening cocktail buffet for friends, a celebration of the birthday person's special "Passages" through life, honoring the wisdom of age, friendship, and accomplishments. At no time and for no reason should the term "over the hill" be used!

*Recipe included in book

Create an invitation that hints at the significance of the event. Find a copy of a newspaper from the day the honoree was born, use pages from an old calendar or magazine, pictures of the celebrant "then" and "now", or a copy of their original birth certificate. Detail plans for the event carefully, particularly if you're hoping for a surprise.

Along with the invitation, send each guest a sheet of special stationery that they can use to construct a page for the birthday memory book — don't forget to include friends from out-of-town or around the world, favorite old teachers, co-workers, distant relatives. Ask to have the pages sent back, full of clippings, photos, poems, memories, a letter, cartoons or cutouts, in plenty of time to be bound as a birthday book. It will be a memorable present, and fun to pour over for many years!

Because of the numbers invited, request that no "real presents" be given. Instead, ask each guest or couple to bring 30 (or 40, or 50, and so on) small items to share — cupcakes, baseball caps, rubber stamps, personalized pens, pizzas . . . the list is endless, and lots of fun! A variation on this number theme is to invite 30 (or 40, or 50. . .) guests and have them each bring their favorite version of a birthday cake. The variety will be remarkable, and can make for clever, edible decor, if space permits!

The menu is planned to satisfy sweet and savory cravings. Finger food is passed on simply garnished trays — less is more in this case — or served from strategically positioned tables. Center the party around the birthday cake and special honoree.

<u>A PUNCH SUGGESTION:</u> A good recipe for Faux Champagne Punch that doesn't require a bottle of bubbly: 1 gallon Rhine wine, 1 pint Brandy, 1½ pints Triple Sec, 3 quarts club soda.

Summer Parties

Formal Breakfast Celebration

A Morning Party for Eight

Family Heritage Day

A Picnic Reunion for Eight to Twenty

Aquatennial Gourmet Picnic by the Lake

An Elegant Picnic for Six to Eight

Grandmother's Yard Party

A Special Outing for Special Friends

Photo Finish

A Picture-perfect Menu for Ten

Lake Harriet

Formal Breakfast Celebration
A Morning Party for Eight

Freshly Squeezed Orange Juice   Champagne

*Baked Eggs with Muenster Cheese

*Rhubarb Muffins and Sweet Butter

*Fresh Strawberries with Raspberry Puree and Pistachio Nuts

Amaretto Coffee

Surely there is a special event in your summer schedule that would be beautifully enjoyed early in the day — a morning party for the bride and groom who won't be married until evening; a surprise honoring a special friend's birthday; a christening celebration; greeting new neighbors, toasting a new business, celebrating your spouse's hard-earned Master's degree. Whatever your reason — maybe you just want to show off a particularly successful season for your rose garden — plan an early party that will start your guests' day off with an elegant flourish.

Note the day's uniqueness by hand delivering invitations — a long stemmed rose or a beautiful helium balloon, tied to a formal handwritten note detailing the day's activity. Encourage guests to dress up in their best garden party finery — this is a day for Dandies and Daisies, reminiscent of Minneapolis' neighbor, St. Paul's most colorful native son, F. Scott Fitzgerald.

Set the table, and the mood, with the best china, polished silver, crystal goblets and pretty, lacy linens. Here is where those days spent poking in antique shops and scouting out estate sales pays off. Create a traditional, formal table, full of special finishing touches that make it all your own.

Enjoy the party out of doors, serving the first toasts of champagne in the garden or from the porch, or sharing the meal from garden chairs and be-linened lap trays.

Baked Eggs with Muenster cheese are the rich choice for an eye-opening entree — their simple preparation and sunny presentation guarantee your own freedom to enjoy the day. Pass lace napkin-lined baskets of Rhubarb Muffins. You might bake these novel goodies in tiny muffin tins or papers, and pass a plate full of sweet butter curls to accompany. Dessert is strawberries, the season's biggest and best, embellished with a pistachio-studded, sparkling raspberry puree, very pretty and nicely light.

Be sure to have plenty of coffee on hand for those not accustomed to early morning libations. Flavored coffee beans lend a party touch even to the coffee pot — amaretto

*Recipe included in book

beans are an especially festive flavor to greet the day.

<u>A WINE SUGGESTION:</u> Mix up a Mimosa: Half orange juice, half champagne.

Family Heritage Day
a Picnic Reunion for Eight to Twenty

Soda, Beer, Lemonade and Iced Tea

Bleu Cheese Spread with Crudites and Crackers

Chips, Pretzels and Cheese Puffs

*Garlic Pepper Steak

Cheeseburgers, Bratwurst, Homemade Rolls for the Kids

*North Country Potato Salad

*Germantown Cole Slaw

*Grapefruit-Avocado Salad with Poppy-Seed Dressing

*Peanut Fudge Ice Cream Bars

*Heavenly Blueberry Pie

Every family should take advantage of the long warm days of summer to plan a party where many generations meet, spend the day together and celebrate their family heritage. Here is a reunion with a twist, to focus on past accomplishments and share future goals, a time to really talk with grandparents and to enjoy the energy of the children.

Invitations can be written out as a letter, describing your hopes for the day, and asking for input from all the family members who will be in attendance. Perhaps you might prepare a questionnaire, asking for special family memories and updates, to be completed and returned before the picnic. With this family information you can prepare a clever family history — even if it's no more complicated than booklets of the questions prepared at the copy shop. Send copies to family elders and those who could not attend and use the "news" to write up a family trivia game.

Ask for photographs and drawings, stories written by and about the family, and any other information that will add to the day's festivities. Draft a VCR cameraperson to record the day's events, and be sure to have a Polaroid camera and lots of film ready. Request a recipe swap of all the family favorite foods — a cherished cookbook might be a project to publish before the next reunion!

If your backyard allows, plan the party for home, or locate a campsite with a shelter

*Recipe included in book

for the party — unfold a large map over one wall and pinpoint every family's "natural habitat." Drawing up a wall-sized family tree is another good idea. Use colored sheets for tablecloths and pass around permanent markers so the tables can be autographed or otherwise personalized into family heirlooms.

Pitchers of flowers can decorate the tables — those planning on a late supper might want to use lanterns or carefully placed candles. Stock the serving tables with a rainbow of paper napkins, heavy paper plates, plastic cutlery, and garbage bags!

Activities for the day will depend on your numbers, special talents, location and energy level — softball, volleyball, frisbees, croquet, sack races and egg tosses, swimming, canoeing, and nature walks are all possible, as long as everyone returns in time for the family feast!

Serve buffet-style from big crocks and wooden bowls. The grown-ups in the group will enjoy the saucy Pepper Steak, but don't be surprised to see them biting into a brat or burger as well! Traditional picnic cole slaw and potato salad take on flavorful new twists in this menu and are joined by a beautiful and fruity green salad tossed with favorite poppy seed dressing.

What's a party without dessert? End the day with a fat wedge of the best Blueberry Pie imaginable or by serving creamy Peanut Fudge Ice Cream Bars. Wrap up the leftovers, if any, while someone strums a banjo for the sing-a-long — a perfect ending to a wonderful day, "family style"!

A WINE SUGGESTION: Fill a galvanized tub full of ice, Beaujolais or Corbieres.

Aquatennial Gourmet Picnic by the Lake
An Elegant Picnic for Six to Eight

Wine, Imported Beers, Champagne

*Cold Watermelon Soup

*Italian Herb Chicken (a Pasta Salad)

*Roast Beef and Avocado Salad

Fresh Tomato Slices

Breadsticks

*Strawberries with Vanilla Sauce

Every summer Minneapolitans take to the lakes with a weeklong celebration of summer, appropriately dubbed "Aquatennial." It is a week of parades and parties, boat races of every craft imaginable, music and fireworks, and lots of picnics — lakeside, of course!

At least once during the summer, plan to pull out all the stops and host a formal picnic complete with damask tablecloth and napkins, the good silver, a candelabra, buffet-sized plates and small glass dessert bowls and a cassette recorder with lots of tapes — Gershwin, Ellington, Sousa and Mozart. Every extra touch and opulent surprise will add to the memorable quality of the party, leaving a feeling that goes far beyond the effort spent polishing the silver, risking the crystal and bleaching some grass stains out of your rarely-used linens.

Invitations can run the gamut from formal printed cards (using nautical summer colors), clever postcards, or to your own lakeside watercolored notes. Ask the revelers to dress up as much as they dare — this is a moment for summertime romantic fantasy. Encourage frilly tea dresses, tuxedos and bare feet!

Outfit your picnic baskets carefully — there's no sadder hostess than one with a vinaigrette soaked pack! Take the little extra time to carry the salads to the site in tape-sealed plastic containers and transfer them to beautiful serving bowls to garnish just before supper is served. The dessert berries must be carried in hard-sided containers, the creamy sauce in a separate jar or taped container.

Cold Watermelon Soup, the first course and a summery surprise itself, tastes best poured from a thermos into pretty punch cups or mugs, and garnished with a slice of kiwi or wedge of lime. The rest of the menu will be at its best at natural temperature, but be

*Recipe included in book

careful to keep the salads cooled if the day's too hot! Pass a napkin-lined basket of the best breadsticks you can muster and paddle some sweet butter into a tiny ramekin to accompany.

Wrap any breakables, including the wine (unless you're planning to ice down a chest full of wine, coolers, seltzers, imported beers and "bubbly" — a good idea for any summerfest!) in the tablecloth, and include a few colorful quilts and blankets to extend your seating area. And by all means, don't forget the corkscrew!

Enjoy the picnic knowing that you've created a memory to cherish for years to come. Lakeside, summerfest, or just a special meal shared with the best of friends, this is a celebration of grand tradition, perfectly suited to our great outdoors.

<u>A WINE SUGGESTION:</u> Italian Pinot Grigio or fruity and light Italian Frascati

Grandmother's Yard Party
A Special Outing for Special Friends

Grandmothers' Menu

*New England Date Bread with Orange Cheese Log

*North Shore Chicken Salad

Fresh Fruit Platter

*Chocolate Chip Cheesecake

Grandchildrens' Menu

Snack tray with Cheerios, cheese cubes and Goldfish crackers

Peanut Butter and Jelly Sandwiches, crusts removed

Apple Slices

Oreo Cookies and Milk

Summer is a time for visiting. Often the favorite trip is the one back home, to share some moments with dear friends and family, and to introduce the younger generation to the place that was once home.

This is the time for grandmothers to gather and plan a picnic for their special offspring. Better than any "brag book," this yard party is designed so that grandmothers can show off their grandchildren in style — and the kids can enjoy a play day, too.

Coordinate the party to fall when the most grandchildren will be in town, but don't overlook the grandmas who don't have visitors at the time. Send invitations that appeal to the child in us all — a teddy bear, a rag doll, an invitation written on a plastic ball or a paper kite. (Remind the grandmothers to pack their cameras!) The party will run over the lunch hour, from eleven to one; please be prompt so that the youngsters can return home in time to take their afternoon naps!

Decorate the yard with bunches of balloons and streamers, and be sure to have all available yard toys on hand for the busy young guests. Tapes of children's music will add to the party atmosphere — try to find some that incorporate games and play activities.

Let the young guests eat first. After they've filled their cheeks, hands and pockets with Cheerios, cheese and Goldfish crackers, send them off to their special picnic table or cloth

*Recipe included in book

with brightly colored miniature shopping bags. Wrap the sandwiches and fruit carefully so they can enjoy fuss-free lunching. Be sure to include plenty of colorful napkins, small cartons of milk or juices, straws and a small package of Oreos for dessert.

Once the children are settled, the grandmothers can enjoy their own repast — oven-fresh date bread spread with a creamy blend of oranges and cheese, a beautiful platter of the season's freshest fruit, and a North Shore version of the chicken salad theme that celebrates our great lakeland grain wild rice

Dessert for the Grandmothers is Chocolate Chip Cheesecake, a rich and creamy cheesecake filled with chocolate mini-chips.

Clear the plates and gather the lunchbags . . . and delegate two grandmas to sneak away and don the costume of clowns or a favorite children's cartoon character. These two can pass around balloons and noisemakers and lead the children in a party-ending parade around the yard.

AN IDEA FOR A PAIR OF PUNCHES: For the Grandma's, mix equal parts of cranberry juice and dry white wine. Children will enjoy a party punch of equal parts cranberry juice and 7-Up.

Photo Finish
A Picture-Perfect Menu for Ten

*Brandy Slush

*Vegetable Pizzas

*Grilled Walleye with Vera Cruz Topping

*Mushroom Rice Pilaf

*Green Salad with Raspberry Vinaigrette

*Strawberry Bavarian Pie

Here is a lighthearted party modeled after the scavenger hunts we all enjoyed as children — only this time it's a grown-up version, using instant-print cameras and a list of clever poses to be "shot," providing countless surprises and activities for a summer's evening.

Your invitation will be the first clue that something out of the ordinary is in store. Send a Polaroid photo of the evening's intended "prize" — a trophy "cup" of junky treasures, dressed-up with flowers — and invite the guests to wear safari gear . . . and comfortable shoes.

Plan to begin the party in plenty of time to enjoy the day's end sunset and to pass around the first batch of Brandy Slushes while the guests gather...and the rules are explained. Please remember to serve non-alcoholic beverages for the designated driver of each vehicle.

The point of the snapshot safari is simple — to create enough Polaroid proof of silly memories to fill a scrapbook to enjoy for years to come. Borrow or rent enough instant cameras to outfit the teams of three or so — making sure to provide enough film for both the required photos and the spontaneous opportunities that are bound to happen. Each team is required to bring home 10 photos, each worth a certain point value; the team with the most points in the end will be declared the winner and have the good fortune to carry home the cup for the season.

The list for required photo bounty might include:
1. All of the team on bikes or roller skates (250)
2. All in a freezer (300)
3. Carrying a bellhop (400)
4. Holding a live lobster (150) Live lobster holding a team member (350)
5. On a golf green with the flag (250)

*Recipe included in book

6. All in a pool at least to your knees (350)

7. Pumping gas for a stranger at a self-serve gas station (the stranger must be in the photo too!) (200)

Continue the list to include activities unique to your community, places having to do with your team-member's occupations, risque dares and local points of interest. There should be about 20 choices for the hunters to choose from — be creative.

The teams need a time limit for their searches — allow them an hour and a half to bring home the winning combinations. Pass trays of colorful Vegetable Pizzas, and more Slushes, as the gallery is reviewed and the winner is chosen. An official team toast can cap the dinner.

Supper is centered around Minnesota's favorite wild flavors — fresh walleye sizzling from the grill and spiced with crunchy Vera Cruz sauce, a side sampling of hearty pilaf, and a wild green salad bowl, tossed with berry dressing. If you can set a proper table near your grill please do so. If you will be picnicking inside, plan to brighten the room with shiny tin cans full of flowers, clever placecards made from film boxes and team photos. The elegant cup can be your centerpiece!

End the evening with rich slices of Strawberry Bavarian Pie — and lay some plans for next year's competition, celebrating a 2nd Annual Event.

A WINE SUGGESTION: California Sauvignon Blanc or French White Graves

Fall Parties

First Day of School Champagne Breakfast

A Morning Celebration for Eight Mothers

An Evening at the Guthrie

A Post Theatre Dessert Party for Six to Eight

A Fireside Chat

An Evening at Home with Friends for Six to Eight

A Family Thanksgiving Feast

A Holiday Party for Ten to Twelve

First Day of School Champagne Breakfast
A Morning Celebration for Eight Mothers

Champagne   Freshly Squeezed Orange Juice

*Warm Shrimp Flan with Riesling Sauce

*Apricot Bread

Bowl of Fresh Melon and Berries

The first day of school holds abundant reason for celebrating. Maybe it's the first day of "freedom" for a young mother, or a final celebration for a mom whose last child will be off to the "U" next year — whatever the age group, gather all your motherly friends for an early morning meeting in honor of your jobs well done.

Get a jump on the teachers and send invitations with a report card format — make sure the mothers know: Attendance is required! If it's possible, arrange to have the children "drop off" their mothers on their way to class. This way you can snap an instant photo portrait of the proud mother and her child — a great memory of a special day.

Guests are greeted by an easel and chalkboard "WELCOME" — another black board might list the menu and the day's "activities." Encourage active involvement — a group aerobics class, a visit to a local art gallery, a mid-day movie . . . or a good long walk! This is the perfect time too, to really organize that Book Club, an opportunity to set a literary example for the kids.

Set your table centered around a big basket of shiny apples and set a pencil box, full of flowers, at each place. Make your placemats out of calendars (make sure to mark those conference days, vacations and holidays), or with maps from the school supply store.

Give each mother a small notebook or pad to spend some time jotting down her thoughts on the day. Tuck these notes away to give to children at a later time, when you can share the feelings of parenting and back-to-school rituals . . . maybe on the day they send their first child off to face the grown-up world of reading, 'riting and, ah, computer interfacing?

After you've toasted the day with a glass of champagne (maybe stirred into a Mimosa, a lighter touch if you're planning to make a day of it!), lead the ladies into the room where your buffet breakfast has been carefully laid. Encourage diners to use trays — school cafeteria style — and to heap their plates with colorful fruits and airy flan. Homemade apricot bread can be timed to pull from the oven, and served while still warm. Try spreading it with butter sweetened with a spoonful or two of apricot, or berry jam. Mix the jam with softened butter, press the spread into a small crock and serve — delicious!

*Recipe included in book

The meal itself should require little attention on the day of the party. Prepare the fruit the day before and chill, garnishing the bowl with sprigs of fresh mint if you like. Brew a big pot of coffee, and pass bright mugs to guests as they arrive. Pop the flan in the oven and stir the sauce one last time, then join your party . . . you've been busy enough, pressing new plaid dresses, packing up knapsacks, and shooing your own children out the door and down the block.

An Evening at the Guthrie
A Post Theatre Dessert Party for Six to Eight

*Dacquoise with Mocha Butter Cream

*Raspberry Cream Torte

*Macadamia Fudge Cake

*Murphy Coffee

Champagne

Over twenty years ago, an English actor by the name of Sir Tyrone Guthrie had what many felt was a wildly eccentric dream. He was determined to build a noteworthy regional repertory theatre in the America "between the coasts," and so set upon finding a city that was willing to take on his ambitious project.

Now built on a hillside that overlooks downtown Minneapolis, the theatre that bears his name is nationally renowned for its progressive productions, and is the proud center of a flourishing arts community.

Each Guthrie season is welcomed by a series of openings, repertory workshops, and excellent touring groups, all designed to enrich the arts community — and to create a social season for hostesses that knows little limit.

One popular idea for theatre season celebrating is a dessert party held after the show as a sweet goodnight, or following a weekend matinee, as a tea befitting Guthrie himself!

Invitations take the form of a "Playbill" announcing that an outstanding production is in the works. Consider including tickets to the show — it's a great way to do your part for audience development, and to introduce your friends to your favorite local talent.

There may not be an easier party for the host and hostess who really want to spend time with their guests. All the setting up can be done in advance, so when you return from the theatre all is in order, down to the coffee, ready to be poured!

Set the buffet table the day before. It is an evening of simple elegance, set off by theatre posters and "Playbills," black dessert dishes and linen napkins, good silver, crystal champagne flutes, spare and beautiful flowers, and candles all around. (An afternoon tea can be equally elegant, only brighter, using a delicate touch with the china, linens and an additional tea set — flowers should be reminiscent of an English country garden.)

If possible, prepare the desserts the day of the party. Don't underestimate the helpfulness of lists, timetables and "delegated duties." Careful organization here is bound to earn you much applause.

*Recipe included in book

Garnish many-leveled cake plates, stands and platters with curls of foil ribbon, fresh fruit or flowers, even a pair of ticket stubs! Cover different sized boxes, or the table itself, with mylar or foil to create an eye-catching table. Offer hot cups of Murphy coffee, spiked with two liqueurs, and pass a big silver bowlful of freshly whipped cream for topping.

Turn on some good old Cole Porter or Gerswhin to set the party mood. Maybe the final toast of the evening with champagne will be a salute to dear friends, fine arts, and the good fortune to share one with the other.

<u>A WINE SUGGESTION</u>: Something a little sweet and very special — Demi Sec Champagne or Italian Asti Spumate.

A Fireside Chat
An Evening at Home with Friends for Six to Eight

*Tomato and Chive Soup

*Veal with Pistachios

*Risotto Milanese

Steamed and Buttered Brussels Sprouts

*Pronto's Rosemary Rolls

*Apple Almond Tart with Whipped Cream

What is nicer on a cool fall night than spending a quiet, cozy evening around the fire, telling stories, playing games, and enjoying a hearty, home-cooked meal?

Here is a party that breaks the rules of a more formal society — dress down, bring a favorite pillow or blanket, forget about the hot, new restaurants in town. Here is a party to share with your most comfortable of friends, and a night dedicated only to celebrating the first fire in the fireplace.

Send an invitation that describes the "broken rules" for the cozy event. Invite friends to come for supper and "a fireside chat," and ask them to bring a game to play, a story to tell, scrapbooks and pictures from summer vacation, a favorite record, a log to throw on the blaze.

Greet your guests with a home that has been sweetly scented by a boiling pot of cinnamon sticks, bay leaves and cloves. Pass hot mugs of Tomato and Chive Soup, bowls of pretzels, popcorn and buttery homemade croutons for "floating" and munching, and their favorite beverage to sip while starting the evening . . . and the fire.

Tuck quilts over the dinner table and make use of beautiful old crocks, wooden bowls and platters. Play up nooks and crannies with tiny arrangements of straw flowers, mums, cattails, baby gourds and pumpkins.

The menu has a foreign flavor but is full of favorite tastes — Veal with Pistachios is a hearty sauté of tender veal, finished with a cream sauce and a nutty crunch of pistachios. It is perfectly accompanied by a comforting mound of Risotto Milanese and crisply steamed Brussel sprouts. Be sure to make plenty of Pronto's Rosemary Rolls, rich herb rolls made popular by a favorite local Italian "ristorante."

Adjourn the diners for a brisk walk through the neighborhood before dessert, or maybe for the first round of charades. Pass the coffee, cream and sugar, and big wedges of

*Recipe included in book

Apple Almond Tart, a celebration of fall's favorite fruit, made all the more luscious with a dollop of freshly whipped cream.

As the fire fades to embers, pack your friends out into the night with a plate of homemade cookies each, thanking them for sharing this final farewell to summer and the chance to warm themselves with the season's first fire.

<u>A WINE SUGGESTION:</u> Something with an earthy appeal — Cotes du Rhone or a hearty Red Zinfandel.

A Family Thanksgiving Feast
A Holiday Party for Ten to Twelve

*Rosemary's Punch

*Grand Marnier Spread with Assorted Sweet Crackers

*Sweet Potato-Pear Casserole

Fresh Buttered Broccoli

Turkey with Homemade Stuffing

*Honey Lemon Whole Wheat Rolls

*Pumpkin Cream Torte

*Cranberry Pecan Pie

What holiday cook isn't looking for a new menu to serve the family when they flock to the year's biggest feast? Here are some variations on a favorite old theme, designed to help create new tastes for a holiday meal to remember.

Thanksgiving is a joyful time for gathering the clan and those special friends to share wonderful community and to count the many blessings of the year that so quickly passed. This celebration is a traditional and often predictable affair, so be sure to take some time to show those close to you that you think they're special. Send everyone a formal invitation to join you in the spirit of the season. A personal note or letter in the mail makes a lovely difference.

Share your love and good fortune. Put together a family food basket and deliver it to a church or station that will see it taking on a family project, volunteering to help serve a meal to the elderly or needy, or working with a program at church. Your blessings will be returned one-hundred-fold.

If your guest list includes an abundance of children, you might want to consider using the tremendous selection of paper party goods available for decorating their places at the table. Try to keep the meal a "family affair," seating little ones in between adults and including them in party conversation. Adults can enjoy "their time" during cocktails and dessert, but dinner is a time to enjoy each other!

This meal is a natural for buffet serving, and the table should be set to allow for easy access to second servings! Make good use of warming trays — stuffing is almost always

*Recipe included in book

best when it's hot! Keep wine and ice water nearby for easy refills. Encourage diners to "eat while it's hot" and save the family prayer until all are seated or before dessert. Placecards and a well-choreographed line up are good ideas too, especially when children are present.

Your centerpiece can be beautiful baskets filled with nuts, fruits and flowers. Fill different sized hollowed pumpkins with dried wildflowers and set them throughout the house. Spray paint small shocks of wheat in colors that coordinate subtly with your holiday decor — add a shake of glitter for an extra special look. And as always, to make it a real party, don't forget to light the candles.

Start the party with a cup of Rosemary's punch, a rosy quencher mixed with the kids in mind. Adults will like a cracker spread with sweet and cheesy Grand Marnier Spread — wheatmeal "cookies" and Bremer wafers are particularly good here.

Stuff and roast the turkey in your favorite manner, but accompany it with some new flavors, perhaps introducing a new family heirloom recipe in the process. Sweet Potato-Pear Casserole adds a smooth new touch and is a perfect compliment to your favorite savory stuffing and tender turkey. Hot and delicious Honey Lemon Whole Wheat Rolls will be good for building those wonderful late-night turkey sandwiches . . . better make a double batch.

Pass a platter of Pumpkin Cream Torte bars and wedges of tart Cranberry Pecan Pie before you push back from the table at last, and count your blessings that such a feast won't happen again for another year . . . or at least until Christmas!

A WINE SUGGESTION: French Vouvray or, closer to home, California French Colombard.

Winter Parties

Festival of Trees

A Progressive Dinner for Five Couples

Starting a Tradition

A New Year's Eve Cross-Country Skiing Party for Eight

Souper Bowl Party

A Football-Watching Supper for Eight to Ten

Dinner in the Orient

Dinner at the Movies for Six to Eight

The Kids are Asleep

A Romantic Dinner for Two

Nicollet Mall

Festival of Trees
A Progressive Dinner for Five Couples

*Old-Fashioned Egg Nog

*Baked Havarti

*Wild Rice Soup

*Festive Romaine Salad

*Ham Braised in Madeira

*Italian Sage Potatoes

*Broccoli Puree

*Raspberry Mousse Meringue Pie

One of the Minneapolis Junior League's most popular fundraising events is the yearly Festival of Trees, an elaborate display of beautiful, designer-decorated holiday trees. It is a favorite tradition anticipated for sharing with family and friends.

By adapting the Junior League idea to a smaller scale, you can enjoy the special season with four or five couples, sharing the beauty of your homes during a progressive dinner party.

No more formal invitation is required than to agree on a date and schedule with the couples involved. Dress in your most comfortable holiday entertaining finery, bring hand-made ornaments to decorate each house's trees, perhaps decorating cookies at one stop, singing carols at another.

All the houses will be decorated in their best holiday look. Break out the Christmas china, special silver and fine crystal — this is a special party! Drape your table in your best cloths; red, green, white, damask and lace — mix them up! Tie the napkins with a sprig of holly or evergreen, and wrap in a favorite saying of the season, a verse, good wishes or a line from a suitable song.

Apples and Christmas pears are always beautiful, mounded into a bountiful center-piece; try piling them high within a grapevine wreath tied with holiday ribbon and accented with baby's breath or evergreen. Light the candles and invite the guests in.

The first stop is for "breaking in the noggin," and imbibing in a traditional holiday brew of eggs, cream and brandy/bourbon. This rich toast is accompanied with easy and

*Recipe included in book

elegant Baked Havarti.

When the group has gathered, point the party in the direction of the second stop, a first course warmer of wild rice soup. This potage holds a special place in Minnesotan hearts and truly celebrates the native grain of its northern waters.

A salad course is next — this one a colorful bowl of romaine and pomegranate. The hostess for this house might prefer to have the salad pre-plated and served formally, perhaps with a toast to the New Year and a flute of chilled champagne?

Dinner is served at House Number Four — a slow basted country ham with a rich Madeira wine flavor. Slice the ham tableside so everyone can enjoy its festive presentation; pass a platter of sage-spiked potatoes and a bowl of colorful broccoli, family style with a formal feeling, extra special when shared with good friends.

One more stop and the evening will be complete — happily ending with a colorful slice of dreamy Raspberry Mousse Meringue Pie.

Share season's greetings over a final cup of coffee and bask in the peace of the season. We think you'll agree — the Festival of Trees is a celebration that bears repeating, year after year!

A WINE SUGGESTION: Schloss Vollarads or elegant Grey Riesling.

Starting a Tradition
A New Year's Eve Cross-Country Skiing Party for Eight

*Holiday Cider Toddy

*Pesto French Bread Slices

*Crocked Cheese with Cognac, Rice Crackers

*Cajun Seafood Stew

*Fresh Greens with Viltoft Dressing

*Cheesy Onion Bread

*Frozen Chocolate Crepes with Butter Rum Sauce

Set this special evening aside to share with your closest friends. In wintry Minnesota this can mean organizing an outing for a silvery evening, and a late night glide on skis to welcome the New Year by the light of the moon!

Create a memorable event by planning a parkside tour close to the home fires. The important thing is to spend the time together with friends — and maybe their whole families — counting your blessings and tracing your growth throughout the challenges of the year past.

Set the mood for the specialness of the evening with your invitation — a box of sparklers (to bring for the party!), or a tiny pair of mittens, tied with a ribbon and carrying a note with all the party details. Remind everyone to dress casually and in many sporting layers — between the skiing and the hot mulled wine there shouldn't be a chill in the house!

Invite the guests to come early for a cocktail and a discussion on what wax to use for the evening's outing. Pass a platter, garnished with evergreen, full of savory Pesto French Bread Slices. Paddle a crockful of cognac-spiked cheese and set it on a board that has been spread with Bremer wafers, rice crackers, Lavosh, and knakkerbrot (a Swedish rye crisp that is a special favorite around these parts).

The table has been set with a red flannel cloth (flannel sheets are ideal for this purpose!) and lumberjack plaid napkins that have been rolled and tied, tucked with more evergreen. The centerpiece will be an old ski boot, made new again with a coat of shiny paint and filled with evergreen, baby's breath and the freshest flowers available.

Set each place with a namecard that also carries a year — guests can share important

*Recipe included in book

events and memories of each year throughout the meal. Serve big bowls of steaming Cajun Stew, hot from the pot on the stove and pass a spicy toss of crisp greens and Viltoft dressing. Baskets of homey Cheesy Onion Bread will provide the diners with savory "dunkers" to swirl in the stew, perfectly accompanied with cool beers, hearty wine, and sparkling seltzers.

Send the skiers out for a moonlight celebration, complete with party hats and horns, sparklers, fireworks and a bottle of champagne. There are bound to be a couple of "station-keepers" who will be happy to assemble the dessert, a heady platter of Butter Rum-sauced Frozen Chocolate Crepes, a final warming toast for when the athletes return and the New Year has officially begun.

A WINE SUGGESTION: Gewurtztraminer or a popular White Zinfandel.

Souper Bowl Party
A Football-Watching Supper for Eight to Ten

*Hot Red Wine Punch

Assorted Cracker Basket

*Harvest Popcorn

*Dijon Sausage Soup

*Cream of Spinach and Clam Soup

*Salad Elaine

*Parmesan Cheese Bread

*Brownie Torte

Obviously based on January's Super Bowl festivities, the football theme is easily adapted for a New Year's Day Bowl game gathering, or a party for parents after high school Homecoming battles.

Minneapolitans are always looking for new recipes when it comes to brewing steaming bowls of hearty soups. There is no better food for soothing winter-chilled bodies and pleasing increasingly creative palates. There is also nothing so easy to prepare! Serve soup when you want to stay out of the kitchen and in with the party!

"Pass" invitations written on a small plastic football or a felt pennant you have stitched yourself. Let your fellow fans know there will be a penalty for late arrival!

Encourage your guests to wear their team colors — jerseys top the list of casual chic. Have a football mum — proper colors and letters, according to the day's match-up — ready to pin on each woman present. Pass around pom-pons, miniature megaphones, victory buttons (all available at local college or sports shops). Divide into teams (heaven help the hostess!), pass big bowls of Harvest Popcorn and go!

Set a buffet-style table with game day balloons, more toy footballs, pom-pons, pennants and a "program" describing the available "concessions."

Halftime is suppertime, with a pair of savory soups sharing the spotlight. Serve mugs of soup (easier to handle in this sporting format) from colorful tureens, or straight from the stove, accompanied by larger, buffet-sized plates for the salad and Parmesan Cheese Bread — a must for dunking. T.V. trays, too, have their place at this party; the important

*Recipe included in book

thing is the guests' comfort and fun, accomplished with as little juggling as possible.

When the cheering ends, celebrate a victory or soothe a defeat with thick slices of a spectacular Brownie Torte, a winner by all accounts, and mugs of coffee. Everyone should agree, it's not whether you win or lose, it's friendship and hearty food that make the game so great.

<u>A WINE SUGGESTION:</u> French Macon or Sonoma Chardonnay.

Dinner in the Orient
Dinner at the Movies for Six to Eight

An assortment of Oriental Beers

*Crabmeat Puffs

*Hot and Sour Soup

*Gingered Pork and Scallions

Fried Rice

*Snow Pea, Mushroom and Red Pepper Salad

*Mandarin Orange Cake

There's nothing that's more entertaining than a movie, particularly when it's a good, old mystery flick with an ending you can't . . . quite . . . remember. We suggest a vintage Charlie Chan mystery, a perfect choice when an Eastern dinner is the order of the day and "whodunit" is on everyone's mind.

Rent a projector and screen — real oldtime movie style — and secure the entertainment of your choice. Projectors, films and all the necessary accessories are available at the local public library; there are times when an evening around the VCR just won't do!

Send "tickets" printed with the party's date, time and address — you can either announce the show and request that guests dress in an appropriate manner, or keep the show a secret until the reel is rolling!

Welcome the movie-goers into your somehow transformed Cinema Palace with Chinese music (also checked out from the library) and decorations with a Far-Eastern feeling. Travel and movie posters should line the walls and if you can find a paper dragon to hang, by all means, this is the time.

Scour local oriental groceries for unusual canned products with beautiful colored labels — these can be stacked into a colorful centerpiece, or emptied out, cleaned and filled with flowers for unique row of clever vases.

Serve the dinner buffet on bamboo trays and be sure to offer chopsticks . . . with forks close at hand for back-up duty! Perhaps you can even purchase a number of paper take-out containers from a nearby chow mein restaurant or paper store — they are available in bright colors (to add to your centerpiece) and can also be used as serving bowls or individual containers. Settle the guests in with their choice of beverage, the

*Recipe included in book

requisite bowls of popcorn, and pass bamboo platters of hot Crabmeat Puffs — accompanied by lots of bright cocktail napkins to accommodate buttery fingers.

When the movie is rolling you can serve hand-held bowls, Chinese style (or even easier, mugs) of spicy Hot and Sour Soup to sip while your guests are guessing who the murderer is.

Stop the movie before the ending is revealed, and keep the viewers in suspense as they enjoy an Oriental banquet of Gingered Pork, colorful Fried Rice and crisp Snow Pea salad.

When dinner is over and the guests have again taken their places for the show, roll the end of the movie — no fair telling the outcome! Film critics and dessert fans alike will enjoy reviewing the evening over Mandarin Orange Cake, spooned with whipped cream and garnished with leftover slices of tiny oranges, and coffee or green tea. This is a perfect opportunity to set up the "schedule" for the next showing of the "film society" — maybe a showing of "Rear Window" and a dinner done "a la 21 Club"!

A WINE SUGGESTION: California Johanisberg Riesling or Oppenheimer Kroten Brunner.

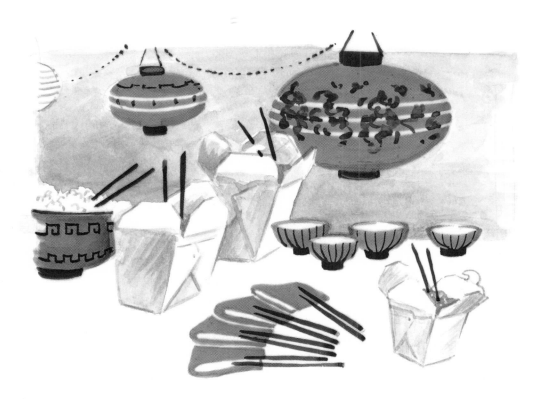

The Kids are Asleep
A Romantic Dinner for Two

Champagne

*Scallops and Avocado with Red Pepper Sauce

*Veal Chops with Sorrel Sauce

Parsley Buttered Noodles

*Squash Puree with Sherry

*Coffee Almond Cream

Every love affair deserves some extra attention every now and then. This romantic supper is designed for taking some special time out, to rekindle old flames — or to ignite new ones! The table has been set for Valentine's Day, a holiday for snuggling here in the North, but the sentiment would be a welcome surprise at any time of the year.

Send your special one a memorable invitation — flowers sent to the office, a telegram, a cassette tape full of favorite music and a spoken invitation to dine, a heart-shaped note on his pillow or in his briefcase. Make the evening a special one for you, too. Call the cleaning service, drop the kids with Grandma, treat yourself to a manicure, haircut, massage or aerobics class. Take a long bubble bath and slip into something that makes you feel beautiful.

Set the table for two and fill the room with flowers and candles. It's a night for ribbons and lace, the good china, your best crystal and a crisp linen cloth.

Dinner a deux is simply assembled. Parslied noodles and a coppery Squash Puree with Sherry can be made ahead and warmed while the cocktails are poured. Veal chops are finished with the flavor of lemony sorrel and the colorful first course is Valentine right with its peppery red sauce.

Freeze Coffee Almond Cream in your prettiest dessert glasses and enjoy their frosty goodness with hot coffee, a favorite late-night liqueur, or a last glass of champagne.

A WINE SUGGESTION: Cotes des Nuits or California Pinot Noir

*Recipe included in book

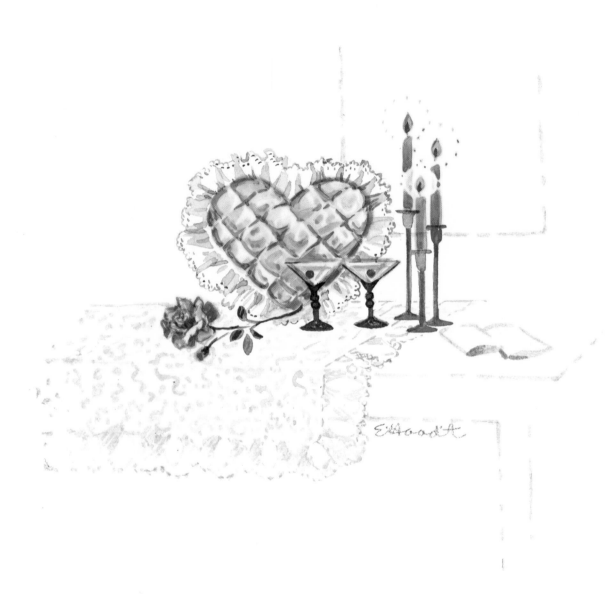

Some Words About Wine

When planning a celebration it's only natural to give some thought to what wine will be served with the meal. While the need for pretense and pricey imports has been outgrown, even a simple glass of wine can turn a rather ordinary meal into a special occasion. Serve wine with confidence: its aromatic flavor will enhance the dinner and improve the guests' palates. Here are some simple guidelines to consider when planning a meal or celebration where wine will add to the festive nature of the event.

WINE GLASSES — If there is one perfect wine glass for all occasions, it is a ten-ounce bowl atop a hand-long stem. This glass will guard the temperature of the wine from the heat of the hand and can be used for everything from sherry to champagne. It is always a correct glass, if not the latest vogue. The worst mistake a person can make when serving wine to guests is to put too much emphasis on the stemware. A fine glass of wine can be enjoyed from a jelly glass just as well as from the finest Baccarat crystal.

Unless you are apt to plan a series of elaborate dinners featuring a wide selection of wines to compliment each course, you will have little use for an extensive collection of stemware. While several glasses set before each place add a certain glittering drama to the impending dinner, they are also difficult to store and maintain. Build your collection with care. One consideration when selecting a set of wine glasses might be to reflect on the importance the sense of smell plays in the appreciation of wine. If you are choosing one glass, pick one with a fairly large bowl to permit the wine drinker to enjoy the bouquet and aroma of the wine.

TASTING WINE — There are five things to look for when tasting wine: First is the color. Very simply, if the wine is clear, it is thought to be good. Secondly, wine is judged by its rich aroma — does it smell like wine? This is not to be confused with the third consideration, that of bouquet. This is a more exacting requirement, describing the type of grape, the time of harvest, and the method of fermenting.

The fourth very pleasant consideration is taste, leading directly to our fifth measuring tool, the aftertaste, which should be mild and good if present at all. If these five observations are good, the wine is fine for serving, regardless of its label or price.

ENTERTAINING IDEAS — The rule to follow here is simple. If you are planning an elaborate dinner, the wine should be fairly expensive. If you are planning a barbecue in the backyard, an inexpensive wine will do.

Most wine shops have competent personnel who are anxious to help choose the right wine to go with your special party. They will help select a wine to compliment the food, whether it's oysters and Chablis, walleyed pike and Muscadet, wild rice stuffed pheasants and California Merlot, or some sweet Port to cut the biting flavor of a tangy wedge of English Stilton.

There is no longer a discrimination when it comes to domestic versus imported wines. Don't be afraid to mix imported wines with the best American food, and don't hestitate to serve a California red with the heartiest "old country" sausage and peppers.

In general, there are only a few dishes to avoid when serving wine as a complement to a meal. Most salads have a vinegar base and are therefore natural enemies for serving with wine. Cheeses, however, have almost a blanket affinity to wine and can be served with little concern for a conflict of flavors.

Some people say "red wine with red meat, white wine with fish or chicken," a general rule, but one that can certainly be deviated from. A better maxim might be to serve a robust wine with a hearty main dish, and a lighter wine with more delicate menus.

Foods that feature elaborate sauces call for careful wine selection, as does highly seasoned food. Preparing chicken in a cream sauce would call for a more delicate wine than would a roast chicken with sage dressing. To go a step further, chicken cooked in wine would probably call for a hearty red wine, while a chicken prepared with a cream sauce is best served by a lighter wine such as a Chardonnay.

It is for this reason that whatever you decide the entree to be, take a hard look at the seasoning and spices in the dish before determining what wine to serve. This, more than the main dish itself, will decide the type of wine to pour. An example here is trout, an oily fish that is best complimented with a very dry white wine to cut through the oiliness. Sole on the other hand is mild and sweet, and is best served by a light white wine.

Be adventuresome when you pair wine with food — serve wines that are appropriate to the regional cooking you are doing, but don't be afraid to go out on a limb. Grilled hamburgers can be easily upgraded when enjoyed with a lovely French Burgundy. Be careful not to be too eclectic — don't cheapen an elaborate veal Orloff with a hastily poured jug red.

The last thing to think about when choosing a wine is the weather. A heavy red wine won't do anything for a meal served on a hot summer night. Consider the setting as well — a lakeside picnic is perfect accompanied by a bottle of white wine chilled in the lake. The time of day is also important. If you are serving lamb for lunch you would serve it with a lighter wine than if you are serving it for dinner.

COOKING WITH WINE — Wine cookery is a far less exotic feat than it sounds. Wine is probably one of the most useful condiments in the cupboard. The important thing to remember is to never cook with a wine you wouldn't drink.

One of the best white wines for sauteing is dry white vermouth, which is actually a wine that has been flavored with herbs and spices. Dry vermouth is handy and delicious, and keeps well in the kitchen; after it has been opened it will last as long as six to eight weeks.

Wine can also be used as a wonderful tenderizer and adds a flavorful dimension to almost any dish. Use sparingly, wine can enrich the flavor of a roast or a holiday turkey. Red wine will add color as well as flavor to a dish, a point to remember when sauteing shellfish or chicken.

Try spooning a couple of tablespoons of wine over half a grapefruit and running it under the broiler for a light dessert. A tablespoon of sherry over a baked apple will have the same special effect.

Wine can enhance almost any dish, from a simple cup of soup to an exotic stir-fry. Madeira mixed with brown sugar and mustard makes a wonderful glaze for a country ham or lamb. Any game dish will benefit from a dash of red wine as it cooks; the wine enzymes will tenderize the meat and add a wonderful flavor to this or any long-simmered meat, roast or stew.

Food and wine have a wonderful relationship to one another. When used properly, wine can add a new dimension to many foods.

John Farrell
Haskells International Wine Room

Beverages

EHoodR

NOTE: As every good host and hostess knows, include a variety of non-alcoholic beverages for you and your guests when entertaining.

Champagne Punch

20 Servings

4 (750-ml) bottles extra dry champagne, chilled
   Juice of 12 lemons (about 2 cups), chilled
¾ cup superfine sugar
1 (750-ml) bottle gin, chilled
   Sliced lemons

Combine all ingredients in punch bowl. Serve with lemon slices.

Celebration Party Punch

12 Servings

2 (750-ml) bottles champagne, chilled
2 cups brandy
1 (6-oz.) can frozen lemonade concentrate, thawed
½ to 1 cup Cointreau or Triple Sec
1 (32-oz.) bottle sparkling water, chilled
   Decorative ice ring or large piece of ice

Combine champagne, brandy, lemonade, liqueur and sparkling water in punch bowl. Float ice in punch.

Bootlegs

12 Servings

1 cup lightly packed fresh mint
1½ cups water
1 (12-oz.) can frozen limeade concentrate, thawed
1 (12-oz.) can frozen lemonade concentrate, thawed
   Juice of 2 lemons
   Juice of 2 limes
   Ice cubes or crushed ice
   Gin, vodka or rum
   Club soda, chilled

Place mint in blender; add water and blend. Let stand 5 minutes. Strain through coarse sieve. Mix concentrates and juices in 2-quart non-metal pitcher. Add mint liquid. To make 1 drink: Fill highball glass with ice. Add 1½ oz. (3 tablespoons) gin, vodka or rum. Add 3 oz. (about ⅓ cup) mint mixture. Fill glass with club soda.

White Sangria with Fresh Fruit

8 Servings

1   (750-ml) bottle dry white wine, chilled
1¼   cups chilled club soda
½   cup Cointreau or Triple Sec
¼   cup sugar
      Whole fresh strawberries or grapes, orange, lemon or lime slices

TIP: *Sangria ingredients can be combined ahead and refrigerated, except for club soda. Add soda just before serving.*

Combine wine, club soda, liqueur and sugar in punch bowl or non-metal pitcher. Add desired amount of fresh fruit. Serve in tall wine glasses, if desired.

Grand Sparkling Punch

16 Servings

1   (750-ml) bottle dry champagne, chilled
2   (32-oz.) bottles ginger ale, chilled
¾   cup Grand Marnier, chilled

TIP: *For an ice ring, freeze thick orange slices in water in ring mold, if desired. Float in punch bowl.*

Combine all ingredients in punch bowl just before serving.

Brandy Slush

8 Servings

Keep plenty on hand for hot weather boating parties and barbecues.

4   black tea bags
2   cups boiling water
6   cups cold water
1½   cups brandy
1½   cups sugar
1   (12-oz.) can frozen lemonade concentrate, thawed
1   (6-oz.) can frozen orange juice concentrate, thawed
      Lemon-lime flavored carbonated beverage, if desired
      Orange slices

Steep tea bags in boiling water about 5 minutes; remove tea bags. Cool tea. Combine remaining ingredients except orange slices with cool tea; freeze in covered container. To serve, thaw to slush consistency; spoon into glasses. Fill with lemon-lime beverage. Garnish with orange slices.

Strawberry Grapefruit Drink

6 Servings

A perfect non-alcoholic offering for brunch.

1 (10-oz.) pkg. frozen strawberries
1 cup grapefruit juice
½ cup sugar
10 to 15 ice cubes

Place all ingredients in blender; whip until smooth. Pour into glasses; garnish with fresh strawberries, if desired.

Rosemary's Punch

20 to 24 Servings

Punch mixture can be frozen; thaw and add ginger ale and fruit just before serving.

　Ice cubes or ring
2 cups chilled orange juice
1 cup chilled lemon juice
1 cup grenadine syrup
6 cups chilled ginger ale
　Orange slices
　Maraschino cherries

Place ice cubes or ring in large punch bowl. Combine orange juice, lemon juice and grenadine; pour over ice. Add ginger ale and fruit; stir to mix.

Holiday Fruit Punch

20 Servings

1 (28-oz.) bottle white grape juice
1 (7-oz.) envelope presweetened strawberry drink mix
1 (6-oz.) can frozen pink lemonade concentrate, thawed
1 (28-oz.) bottle ginger ale
2 (28-oz.) bottles club soda

Refrigerate all ingredients until chilled; combine in punch bowl.

Old-Fashioned Egg Nog

28 Servings

This recipe is over 50 years old.

12 egg yolks, beaten until very thick
11 tablespoons sugar
2 cups bourbon
2 cups dark rum
2 cups milk
1 quart whipping cream
2 cups milk
½ cup peach brandy
Whipped cream
Nutmeg

Combine egg yolks, sugar, bourbon, rum and 2 cups milk; let stand 15 minutes. Stir in cream, 2 cups milk and brandy. Refrigerate 2 to 3 days. Serve topped with whipped cream and a sprinkle of nutmeg.

Holiday Cider Toddy

20 to 30 Servings

Wonderful aroma! This is good to serve on a cool fall evening.

TIP: *Toddy can also be made in a large heavy saucepan; simmer 15 to 20 minutes. Do not boil.*

2 quarts apple cider
1 (48-oz.) bottle cranberry juice cocktail
½ cup packed brown sugar
1½ teaspoons whole cloves
½ teaspoon salt
4 cinnamon sticks
1 (750-ml) bottle rosé wine

Combine cider and cranberry juice in 30-cup percolator. Place brown sugar, cloves, salt and cinnamon sticks in percolator basket. Perk; remove basket. Add wine. Serve hot with additional cinnamon sticks, if desired.

Orange Strawberry Cocktail

6 Servings

1 (6-oz.) can frozen orange juice concentrate, thawed
1 quart fresh strawberries, halved
   Sugar
   Fresh mint leaves

Prepare orange juice as directed on can; chill. Puree strawberries until smooth; strain and chill. (Sweeten berries with sugar if necessary.) To serve, fill wine glasses ¾ full with orange juice. Pour strained strawberry juice over orange juice. (Strawberry juice should form a layer over orange juice.) Garnish with mint.

Hot Red Wine Punch

20 Servings

Festive served in a silver punch bowl.

1 cup sugar
½ cup water
4 cinnamon sticks
2 lemons, sliced
5 cups dry red wine
2½ cups pineapple juice
2½ cups orange juice
1 cup dry sherry
½ cup lemon juice

TIP: *Syrup can be made ahead and refrigerated until ready to use. Heat with wine mixture.*

Combine sugar, water, cinnamon sticks and 3 lemon slices in saucepan. Heat to boiling; boil 5 minutes. Strain; set syrup aside. Combine remaining ingredients in large saucepan. Heat thoroughly; do not boil. Add syrup and remaining lemon slices. Serve hot.

Murphy Coffee

1 to 2 Servings

Minnetonka Mist, Spring Park, is a fun restaurant located on Lake Minnetonka.

8 to 10 oz. prepared hot coffee
¾ oz. Kahlua
¾ oz. Bailey's Irish cream liqueur
   Sweetened whipped cream

Combine coffee, Kahlua and liqueur. Pour into coffee mugs. Garnish with whipped cream.

Appetizers and First Courses

Pepperoni Bread

*8 Appetizer Servings
(3 to 4 Main Course Servings)*

*Especially popular with
teen-agers.*

1 (1-lb.) loaf frozen bread dough, thawed
½ teaspoon dried parsley flakes
¼ teaspoon dried oregano leaves, crushed
¼ teaspoon garlic powder
¼ teaspoon seasoned salt
3 tablespoons butter or margarine, melted
1 (3½-oz.) pkg. thin-sliced pepperoni, quartered
8 oz. (2 cups) shredded Provolone cheese

Heat oven to 350°F. Roll dough to 12 x 9-inch rectangle on lightly floured surface. Combine seasonings with butter; brush lightly on dough, reserving some for top of dough. Cover with pepperoni slices, then with cheese. Roll up jelly-roll style. Brush with remaining butter mixture. Pinch seams of dough tightly. Place on lightly greased cookie sheet. Bake at 350°F. for about 30 minutes. Cool at least 15 minutes. Cut into 1-inch thick slices.

Sausage and Leek Tarts

48 Appetizers

*We Cater to You, Golden
Valley, Duane and Julie Wade*

*Duane and Julie Wade are the
owners of We Cater to You, a
professional catering firm in
the Twin Cities.*

2 (12-oz.) pkg. pork sausage (1 regular; 1 hot)
3 leeks
¾ cup chicken stock
⅓ to ½ cup whipping cream
2 (1-lb.) loaves thin-sliced sandwich bread
1½ cups butter or margarine, melted

Brown sausage in large skillet until no longer pink; drain well. Wash leeks well and discard green tops. Slice leeks; place in saucepan with chicken stock; heat to boiling. Reduce heat; simmer 5 minutes. Combine leeks, stock, cream (start with ⅓ cup) and sausage in food processor; process until no big pieces remain. Cool; cover and refrigerate up to 3 days or freeze.

TOAST CUPS: Heat oven to 350°F. Cut bread into rounds with 2 to 2½-inch round or fluted cutter. (Should get 2 rounds from each slice; do not use crusts.) Press bread between palms and carefully fit into miniature muffin pans. Brush round generously with melted butter. Bake at 350°F. for 15 to 20 minutes or until crisp and golden. Remove from pans; cool. May be frozen or stored in cool dry place. To serve, spoon sausage mixture (thaw completely if frozen) into toast cups. Bake on cookie sheets in preheated 350°F. oven for about 15 minutes or until thoroughly heated.

Crispy Chicken Wings with Sesame

20 Servings

⅓ cup soy sauce
2 tablespoons honey
2 tablespoons cider vinegar
1 tablespoon minced peeled gingerroot
1 tablespoon sesame oil
2 cloves garlic, minced
¼ teaspoon cayenne pepper
3 lb. chicken wings
3 tablespoons sesame seeds

TIP: *Can be baked 1 day ahead; refrigerate, covered. Reheat at 350°F. for 10 to 15 minutes.*

Combine soy sauce, honey, vinegar, gingerroot, sesame oil, garlic and cayenne in large bowl. Add chicken wings, stirring to coat. Cover and marinate 2 hours at room temperature or overnight in refrigerator. Stir occasionally. Pour into 13 x 9-inch baking dish; sprinkle with sesame seeds. Bake at 425°F. for 30 minutes or until golden and tender. If desired, broil 2 inches from heat for 1 to 2 minutes to crisp skin. Serve warm or at room temperature.

Pesto-Stuffed Mushrooms

8 Servings

If serving as appetizer, use small mushrooms. If serving as first course or accompaniment, use medium to large mushrooms.

TIP: *Mushrooms can be stuffed 3 to 4 hours in advance; refrigerate until time to bake.*

24 fresh mushrooms, stems removed and reserved
1 lemon, halved
Olive oil
¾ to 1 cup Pesto Sauce (page 64)
½ cup grated Parmesan cheese

Heat oven to 375°F. Brush 15 x 10-inch jelly roll pan with oil. Rub mushrooms with lemon to prevent darkening; brush with olive oil. Finely chop reserved mushroom stems; combine with pesto sauce. Fill mushrooms with pesto mixture; sprinkle generously with Parmesan cheese. Arrange mushrooms in prepared pan; drizzle with oil. Bake at 375°F. for 10 minutes or until bubbly.

Wall Street Mussels with White Wine

4 Appetizer Servings
(2 First Course Servings)

Fresh mussels should be scrubbed and the small tuft of hair or "beard" removed. Soak in cold water 1 to 2 hours to remove sand before cooking.

½ cup chopped shallots or scallions
1 clove garlic, minced
⅛ teaspoon dried oregano leaves, crushed
¼ cup butter or margarine
½ cup dry white wine
2 bay leaves
3 quarts mussels, scrubbed and debearded
   Fresh parsley sprigs
1 loaf French bread

Combine shallots, garlic, oregano and butter in large skillet; saute until golden. Add wine and bay leaves; heat 2 minutes. Add mussels; cover lightly. Cook over high heat, shaking pan occasionally, until shells open, about 7 to 8 minutes. Remove bay leaves. Pour mussels and sauce into heated bowls. Garnish with parsley. Serve with French bread for dipping.

TIP: *If mussel shells do not open after cooking, they should be discarded.*

Feta Shrimp Triangles

40 Triangles

4 (5 to 6-inch) pita breads
   Unsalted butter, softened
8 oz. Feta cheese, crumbled
8 oz. baby shrimp or medium shrimp, chopped
2 large cloves garlic, minced
½ cup mayonnaise
½ teaspoon chili powder
½ teaspoon ground cumin
   Sesame seeds
   Paprika

Heat oven to 300°F. Slice pitas in half horizontally. Spread each half with butter; cut into 5 or 6 triangles. (If bread is large, cut into 8 to 10 triangles.) Place on cookie sheet. Bake at 300°F. for 15 to 20 minutes or until lightly browned. Combine Feta cheese, shrimp, garlic, mayonnaise, chili powder and cumin; mix with fork until blended. Spread topping generously on toasted triangles. Sprinkle tops with sesame seeds and paprika. Place on broiler pan; broil 4 to 6 inches from heat until tops are brown and bubbly. Watch closely.

TIP: *Triangles can be made ahead and frozen. To serve, reheat on cookie sheet at 450°F. for 5 to 10 minutes or until heated through.*

Parmesan Mushrooms with Grapes

20 Appetizers

Freshly grated Parmesan makes a world of difference in any recipe. It can be easily grated in a food processor.

20   medium fresh mushrooms
20   seedless green grapes
 2   (5-oz.) pkg. herb and garlic cheese, softened
 ½   cup unsalted butter, melted
 1   cup grated Parmesan cheese
     Freshly ground pepper

Heat oven to 400°F. Remove stems from mushrooms. Place a grape in each cap. Mound ½ tablespoon of herb and garlic cheese over each mushroom, completely enclosing grape. Roll each mushroom in melted butter, then Parmesan cheese. Reserve extra cheese that does not adhere. Place mushrooms in ungreased 15 x 10-inch jelly roll pan; refrigerate 20 minutes. Bake at 400°F. for 15 minutes. Remove from oven; sprinkle with remaining Parmesan cheese. Top with black pepper.

TIP: *A jelly roll pan or sided dish is a must to prevent butter from dripping in oven.*

Grand Marnier Spread

2 Cups

Crisp ginger snaps or fresh fruit or banana nut bread are a nice alternative to crackers.

 2   (8-oz.) pkg. cream cheese, softened
 1   to 2 tablespoons sugar
 2   tablespoons Grand Marnier
 1   tablespoon finely grated orange peel
 ¼   teaspoon orange extract, if desired

Combine all ingredients in small bowl; mix until well blended. Pour into small crock or jar; cover and refrigerate. Serve at room temperature with sweet crackers.

Mexican Cream Cheese Spread

12 to 16 Servings

A delicious change from layered taco dip.

 1   (8-oz.) pkg. cream cheese, softened
 1   cup dairy sour cream
 8   oz. (2 cups) shredded hot pepper cheese
 1   (7-oz. can) ripe olives, drained and sliced
 2   green onions, chopped
 1   (2-oz.) jar pimiento, drained and diced
     Tortilla chips

Beat cream cheese and sour cream together. Stir in shredded cheese, olives, onions and pimiento. Place in serving dish. Serve with tortilla chips.

Crabmeat Puffs

20 Appetizers

Leeann Chin Chinese Cuisine, Minneapolis, Leeann Chin

Leeann Chin is a notable Twin Cities' restauranteur and authority on Chinese cooking.

1 (6 oz.) pkg. frozen crabmeat, drained and cartilage removed, chopped
2 (3-oz.) pkg. cream cheese, softened
½ teaspoon salt
¼ teaspoon garlic powder
40 wonton skins
1 egg, slightly beaten
  Vegetable oil

Combine crabmeat, cream cheese, salt and garlic powder. Brush wonton skin with egg. Place heaping teaspoonful crabmeat mixture in center of wonton skin. (Cover remaining skins with dampened towel to keep them pliable.) Top with another wonton skin; press edges to seal. Brush dab of egg on center of each side of puff. Make a pleat on each edge, pressing to seal. Repeat with remaining wonton skins. (Cover puffs with dampened towel or plastic wrap to keep them from drying out.) Heat vegetable oil (1½-inches) in wok to 350°F. Fry 4 or 5 puffs at a time until golden brown, turning 2 or 3 times, about 2 minutes. Drain on paper towel.

Pesto French Bread Slices

8 Servings

PESTO SAUCE

2 cups fresh basil leaves
2 cloves garlic
¾ cup grated Parmesan cheese
½ cup pine nuts
⅔ cup olive oil

1 loaf French bread
½ cup unsalted butter, softened
1 teaspoon garlic salt
½ cup grated Parmesan cheese

TIPS: *Bread slices can be assembled ahead and refrigerated up to 12 hours; bring to room temperature before broiling.*

Pesto sauce can also be served on pasta or used as filling for Pesto-Stuffed Mushrooms (page 61).

SAUCE: Place basil and garlic in food processor or blender; process until mixture is pureed. Add ¾ cup Parmesan cheese and pine nuts; continue to process until smooth. With processor running, slowly add oil and process until well combined. If too thick, blend in a little water; set aside.

Slice French bread into ¼ to ½-inch slices. Combine butter and garlic salt; spread on bread. Spread ½ to ¾ cup pesto sauce over buttered bread and sprinkle with ½ cup Parmesan cheese. Place bread slices on cookie sheet. Broil 4 to 6 inches from heat for 3 to 4 minutes or until cheese melts and is brown. Serve immediately.

Steak 'n Dip Appetizer

8 to 12 Servings; 1 cup dip

Rare roast tenderloin of beef makes this recipe exceptional.

1   cup mayonnaise
2   tablespoons snipped fresh parsley
2   tablespoons capers
2   tablespoons chili sauce
2   teaspoons Dijon mustard
1   clove garlic
.9 oz. envelope meat marinade mix
2   lb. beef family steak, 1 inch thick

Combine mayonnaise, parsley, capers, chili sauce, mustard and garlic in food processor or blender; blend 30 seconds. Place in small bowl; cover and refrigerate 1 hour. Marinate and cook meat according to marinade package directions; cut into cubes. Serve meat on a bed of leafy lettuce garnished with cherry tomatoes if desired. Serve sauce in separate bowl for dipping.

Sausage Puffs

6 to 8 Servings

Very popular appetizer, Hearty but still finger food

2   (12-oz.) pkg. bulk sausage (1 regular and 1 hot)
4   oz. (1 cup) shredded Swiss cheese
1   tablespoon grated Parmesan cheese
3   eggs, well beaten
1   tablespoon dried parsley flakes
1   teaspoon dried basil leaves, crushed
1   teaspoon garlic powder
    Salt and pepper to taste
1   (17¾-oz.) pkg. frozen puff pastry, thawed
½   cup Dijon mustard
2   tablespoons honey

Heat oven to 350°F. Brown sausage in large skillet; drain and cool. Add cheeses, eggs (reserve 2 tablespoons) and seasonings to sausage; stir gently. Keep pastry very cold until ready to use. Roll out 1 sheet of pastry to 12 x 17-inch rectangle. Place half of sausage mixture along one side of rectangle. Bring sides together by rolling over. Pinch ends tightly. Repeat with remaining pastry and sausage. Place on cookie sheet and form semi-circle. Brush with reserved egg. Bake at 350°F. for 30 to 40 minutes or until golden brown. Cool 10 minutes; slice into 1½-inch slices. Combine mustard and honey; serve with puffs.

Baked Havarti

4 to 6 Servings

1 (1-inch) thick round havarti cheese (approx. 1 lb.)
1 sheet frozen puff pastry
2 tablespoons Dijon mustard
1 to 2 teaspoons dried mixed herbs (fines herbes and dill weed)
   Fresh parsley sprigs

TIP: *Can be assembled and refrigerated until time to bake.*

Heat oven to 375 °F. Thaw pastry 20 minutes; roll out 2 inches larger than cheese round. Combine mustard and herbs; spread on top of cheese. Place cheese top down in middle of pastry. Fold pastry over cheese and tightly seal all edges together. Bake, sealed side down, on cookie sheet at 375 °F. for 30 to 40 minutes. Cool 30 minutes before serving. Cut with sharp knife; garnish with parsley.

Escargot-Stuffed Mushrooms

48 Appetizers

Fitzgerald's, St. Paul, Tom Robertson

This appetizer is easy to prepare with canned escargot.

FILLING

½ lb. butter or margarine
½ teaspoon Dijon mustard
1 teaspoon lemon juice
1½ tablespoons garlic powder
1 egg
¼ cup snipped fresh parsley
1 cup minced green onion

48 small to medium mushrooms, stems removed
48 escargot, rinsed and drained
¼ cup grated Parmesan cheese
4 oz. thinly sliced Swiss cheese, cut into small squares

FILLING: Whip butter until fluffy in food processor. Add mustard, lemon juice, garlic powder, egg, parsley and green onion; process until well blended. Cover and refrigerate.

To serve, heat oven to 400 °F. Scoop butter with melon ball cutter and place 1 ball in each mushroom cap; top each butter ball with 1 escargot. Sprinkle with Parmesan cheese; top each with 1 square of Swiss cheese. Bake at 400 °F. for 10 minutes; then broil until cheese melts and browns lightly. Watch carefully.

Avocado Supreme

12 to 16 Servings

1 envelope unflavored gelatin
¼ cup cold water

EGG LAYER

4 hard-cooked eggs, chopped
½ cup mayonnaise
¼ cup minced fresh parsley
1 large green onion, minced
  Dash hot pepper sauce
  Freshly ground white pepper

AVOCADO LAYER

1 medium ripe avocado, pureed just before adding
1 medium ripe avocado, diced just before adding
1 large shallot, minced
2 tablespoons fresh lemon juice
2 tablespoons mayonnaise
½ teaspoon salt
  Dash hot pepper sauce
  Freshly ground black pepper

SOUR CREAM AND ONION LAYER

1 cup dairy sour cream
¼ cup minced onion

1 (3½ to 4-oz.) jar black or red caviar
  Fresh lemon juice
1 loaf thinly sliced pumpernickel bread

Line bottom of 1-quart souffle dish with foil extending 4 inches beyond rim of dish on 2 sides. Oil lightly. Soften gelatin in cold water in measuring cup. Liquefy gelatin by setting cup in pan of hot water or microwave about 20 seconds at lowest setting. Stir until gelatin is dissolved.

EGG LAYER: Combine all egg layer ingredients with 1 tablespoon of gelatin mixture. Season to taste. Neatly spread egg mixture into prepared dish, using spatula to smooth top. Wipe away any egg mixture from sides of foil.

AVOCADO LAYER: Combine all avocado layer ingredients with 1 tablespoon gelatin mixture. Adjust seasonings to taste. Carefully spread mixture over egg layer.

SOUR CREAM AND ONION LAYER: Combine sour cream, ¼ cup onion and remaining 2 tablespoons gelatin mixture. Carefully spread over avocado layer. Cover dish lightly with plastic wrap; refrigerate several hours or overnight. Just before serving, place caviar in fine sieve and rinse gently under cold running water. Sprinkle with lemon juice; drain. Lift mold out of dish using foil extensions as handles. Remove foil; place mold on serving platter. Spread caviar over top of mold. Serve with bread.

TIP: *Caviar is a delightful finishing touch but it can be omitted.*

Asparagus in Mini Crepes

18-24 Appetizers

We Cater to You, Golden Valley, Duane and Julie Wade

CREPES

3 eggs
1 cup all-purpose flour
¾ cup milk
¾ cup water
¼ teaspoon salt
2 tablespoons butter or margarine, melted

FILLING

1 (8 oz.) pkg. cream cheese, softened
1 clove garlic, minced
¼ cup snipped fresh parsley
Dash dried basil leaves, crushed
Dash dried thyme leaves, crushed
½ teaspoon salt

1 lb. fresh asparagus

CREPES: Beat eggs; blend in flour. Whisk in milk, water, ¼ teaspoon salt and butter. Let stand 1 hour at room temperature or overnight in refrigerator. Whisk batter before use. Heat crepe or omelette pan until drop of water dances on pan surface. Pour small amount of batter into pan. Quickly tilt pan to spread batter. Turn crepe when lightly browned. ("Spotty" side is inside of crepe.) Cut circles from crepes with 3-inch fluted cookie cutter. Cool crepes completely and refrigerate or freeze until needed.

FILLING: Combine all filling ingredients in food processor; blend well.

Peel asparagus; use only tip end. Blanch until tender-crisp; immediately cool in ice water. Drain and refrigerate. (Asparagus can be prepared 24 hours in advance of serving.)

To serve: Spread crepe with a thin layer of cheese mixture; roll around asparagus tip.

TIP: Can be prepared 1 hour before serving; refrigerate.

Bleu Cheese-Stuffed Shrimp

8 Servings

These are beautiful passed on a silver tray. Garnish with lemon and sprigs of fresh dill.

TIPS: Shrimp can be prepared 3 to 4 hours in advance. Filling can also be used to stuff fresh pea pods; omit parsley.

1 (3-oz.) pkg. cream cheese, softened
1 oz. bleu cheese, crumbled
½ teaspoon prepared mustard
1 teaspoon finely chopped green onion
¾ cup chopped fresh parsley
24 jumbo shrimp, cooked, peeled and deveined

Combine cream cheese, bleu cheese, mustard and onion in small bowl. Slit shrimp down back and stuff with small amount of cheese mixture. Carefully roll shrimp in parsley; refrigerate for at least 1 hour.

Vegetable Pizzas

24 Appetizers

Looks very healthy! A popular appetizer.

TIP: *Food processor works well for chopping vegetables. Any assortment of fresh vegetables can be used.*

1 (8-oz.) can refrigerated crescent rolls
1 (8-oz.) pkg. cream cheese, softened
½ cup mayonnaise
1 teaspoon garlic salt
½ teaspoon dried dill weed
½ cup shredded or chopped carrots
½ cup shredded or chopped radishes
½ cup chopped green pepper
¼ cup chopped fresh mushrooms

Heat oven to 350°F. Unroll dough into 2 long rectangles. Overlap long sides to form 13 x 7-inch rectangle on ungreased cookie sheet; firmly press perforations to seal. Bake at 350°F. for 10 minutes. Loosen from cookie sheet; cool. While dough is cooling, combine cream cheese, mayonnaise, garlic salt and dill weed. Spread rolls with cheese mixture. Refrigerate several hours. Before serving spread vegetables on cheese mixture. Cut into squares; place on serving platter.

Scallops and Avocado with Red Pepper Sauce

12 Servings

A colorful and elegant first course

1½ lb. red bell peppers
2 tablespoons olive oil
Salt and white pepper
Cayenne pepper
1½ lb. sea scallops, rinsed and sliced horizontally
½ cup fresh lemon juice
Salt and white pepper
3 large ripe avocados
Lemon juice

Heat broiler. Arrange peppers on broiler pan; broil 6 inches from heat, turning frequently for 10 to 15 minutes or until skins are blistered and charred. Place peppers in paper bag; close and let stand until peppers are cool to touch. Over a bowl, remove and discard skin, seeds and stems of peppers; reserve juice. Puree peppers with juice in food processor or blender. With motor running, add oil and salt, pepper and cayenne to taste; blend until smooth. Transfer to bowl; cover and refrigerate. Combine scallops, ½ cup lemon juice, salt and white pepper to taste in glass bowl; toss until blended. Cover tightly; refrigerate several hours or overnight. Drain scallops. Steam until opaque; drain and refrigerate. Peel, quarter lengthwise and pit avocados. Slice each avocado quarter, keeping one end attached. Brush with lemon juice. Divide sauce onto 12 salad plates; place 1 avocado quarter on each plate, arranging in a fan shape on top of sauce. Top with scallops.

Phyllo Nests with Artichokes and Escargot

6 Servings

Lovely as a first course for a formal dinner.

PHYLLO NESTS

½ cup unsalted butter
6 cloves garlic, minced
6 sheets frozen phyllo dough, thawed
6 tablespoons fine dry bread crumbs

FILLING

4 artichoke bottoms, coarsely chopped
2 tablespoons lemon juice
3 tablespoons minced onion
1 clove garlic, minced
6 tablespoons unsalted butter
2 tablespoons snipped fresh parsley
1 tablespoon Dijon mustard
½ teaspoon Worcestershire sauce
1 (7½-oz.) can escargot, rinsed, patted dry and minced
   Bread crumbs
2 tablespoons unsalted butter

PHYLLO NESTS: Heat oven to 325 °F. Butter 9-inch round cake pan. Melt ½ cup butter with 6 cloves garlic in small saucepan. Brush 1 sheet phyllo dough with garlic butter; sprinkle with 1 tablespoon bread crumbs. (Keep remaining sheets of phyllo dough covered with damp towel.) Using a skewer or chopstick as a guide, loosely roll up phyllo, beginning with short side, ending within 2 inches of opposite side. Crimp phyllo tube together by pushing it toward the center from both ends. Remove skewer. Form the tube into nest by using unrolled phyllo to form bottom of nest. Place nest in prepared pan. Form 5 more nests; place in pan and brush all with remaining garlic butter. Bake at 325 °F. for 20 to 25 minutes or until golden; remove from oven. Increase oven temperature to 450 °F.

FILLING: Toss artichokes with lemon juice to prevent discoloring. Saute onion and 1 clove garlic in 6 tablespoons butter until onion is soft. Stir in parsley, mustard, Worcestershire sauce and escargot. Drain artichokes and add to mixture. Mound mixture in phyllo nests. Sprinkle with additional bread crumbs and dot with remaining butter. Bake nests at 450 °F. for 8 minutes or until tops are golden.

TIP: *Nests can be prepared and baked ahead of time. Do not fill until ready to serve.*

Herb-Marinated Mozzarella

1   lb. Mozzarella cheese, sliced ¼-inch thick with serrated knife
3   tablespoons extra-virgin olive oil
3   tablespoons vegetable oil
1   to 2 tablespoons sliced green onion
1   tablespoon minced and drained bottle sun-dried tomatoes, plus
        1 teaspoon of the oil
½   teaspoon red pepper flakes
1   tablespoon snipped fresh parsley
1   tablespoon snipped fresh basil leaves
1   teaspoon snipped fresh chives
½   teaspoon garlic salt

In wide shallow serving dish arrange overlapping slices of Mozzarella. In small bowl whisk together remaining ingredients; drizzle over Mozzarella. Marinate, covered, at room temperature 2 hours. Serve at room temperature, garnished with fresh herbs, if desired.

Bacon-Wrapped Shrimp

CHILI DIP

1   hard-cooked egg, chopped
¾   cup mayonnaise
3   tablespoons diced sweet pickle
1   tablespoon diced stuffed olives
1   tablespoon chili powder
1½ teaspoons grated onion

SHRIMP

1   lb. fresh shrimp, cooked, peeled and deveined
8   to 10 slices bacon
½   cup butter or margarine, melted
1½ teaspoons chili powder
1   clove garlic, minced

DIP: Combine all ingredients for dip. Cover; refrigerate for at least 1 hour.
   SHRIMP: Wrap each shrimp with ½ slice bacon; refrigerate. Combine butter, 1½ teaspoons chili powder and garlic. Brush shrimp with butter mixture; place on broiler pan. Heat broiler; broil about 3 inches from heat for about 5 minutes on each side or until bacon is well done. Baste with butter mixture several times during broiling. Serve hot with chili dip.

Cinnamon-Glazed Pecans

1 Pound Nuts

Great for holiday gift-giving!

1 egg white
1 tablespoon water
1 lb. pecan halves
1 cup sugar
1½ teaspoons salt
1 teaspoon cinnamon

Heat oven to 300°F. Beat egg white in 1-quart bowl until stiff. Fold water and pecans into egg white. Combine sugar, salt and cinnamon. Sprinkle over pecan mixture; mix well. Spread on non-stick or foil-lined cookie sheet. Bake at 300°F. for 30 minutes. Remove from oven; stir to separate pecans. Cool. Store tightly covered.

Harvest Popcorn

10 Cups

8 cups popped corn
1 cup dry roasted peanuts or mixed nuts
1 cup sesame sticks or canned French fried onions
¼ to ½ cup butter or margarine, melted
1 tablespoon dried dill weed
2 teaspoons Worcestershire sauce
½ to 1 teaspoon garlic powder

Combine popped corn, nuts and sesame sticks or onions in large bowl. Combine remaining ingredients in small bowl; drizzle over popcorn and toss to mix.

Fresh Mushroom Pâté

1½ Cups

Delicious served on water crackers. Garnish with parsley and sliced fresh mushrooms.

1   lb. fresh mushrooms, sliced
2   tablespoons unsalted butter
1   tablespoon dry sherry
4   oz. semi-soft herb and garlic cheese
4   oz. cream cheese
¼   teaspoon salt
    Crackers

TIP: *Pâté can be refrigerated, covered, up to 10 days.*

Saute mushrooms in butter and sherry until almost all liquid has evaporated, 5 to 10 minutes. Combine mushrooms, cheeses and salt in food processor or blender. Blend thoroughly until mushrooms are finely chopped. Pour into cheese crock or serving dish; refrigerate at least 3 hours. Serve at room temperature with crackers.

Cheese-Stuffed Peppers

8 Servings (24 Pieces)

PEPPERS

1   (8-oz.) pkg. cream cheese, softened
2   tablespoons milk
8   oz. (2 cups) shredded Cheddar cheese
¼   cup drained sweet pickle relish
1   teaspoon Worcestershire sauce
1   cup chopped radishes
4   small green peppers, halved and seeded

DIPPING SAUCE

½   cup mayonnaise
½   cup dairy sour cream
1   tablespoon prepared horseradish
½   teaspoon sugar
½   teaspoon salt
2   teaspoons dried dill weed (or to taste)

PEPPERS: Combine cream cheese and milk; blend in Cheddar cheese, relish, Worcestershire sauce, salt and radishes. Stuff cheese mixture into peppers. Cover with plastic wrap and refrigerate several hours or overnight. Just before serving, cut each green pepper half into thirds, lengthwise. Serve on platter surrounding bowl of dipping sauce.
SAUCE: Combine all sauce ingredients.

Crocked Cheese with Cognac

10 to 12 Servings

Delicious served with rice crackers and green grapes or other fruit or seasoned breadsticks. Especially good with a nice bottle of Chardonnay.

TIP: *Experiment with a variety of tangy mustards.*

1   lb. (4 cups) shredded sharp Cheddar cheese
¾   teaspoon curry powder
¼   cup snipped fresh chives
2   tablespoons cognac
2   tablespoons butter, softened
1   tablespoon Pommery or Dijon mustard
     Rice crackers

Combine cheese, curry powder and chives in medium bowl. Gradually blend in cognac, butter and mustard. Mix until spreadable. Pack into crock; seal tightly and refrigerate. Bring to room temperature before serving. Serve with rice crackers.

Wild Rice-Stuffed Snow Pea Pods

20 to 30 Appetizers

An elegant hors d'oeuvre to serve for a special party.

TIP: *Best made 4 to 6 hours before serving. Filling can be made 24 hours in advance and refrigerated. Fill pea pods before serving.*

1   lb. fresh snow pea pods
4   cups cooked wild rice, chilled
½   cup golden raisins
⅓   cup pine nuts, toasted
⅓   cup mayonnaise
⅓   cup dairy sour cream
½   teaspoon curry powder
     Salt to taste

Remove strings from pea pods; slit string side of pods to open. Blanch 1 minute; rinse in cold water. Combine chilled wild rice with remaining ingredients. Fill pea pods with wild rice mixture; refrigerate until serving time.

Hot Mustard Sauce

1½ Cups

Sauce can also be used for appetizers, as a spread for sandwiches or as a dip. A nice accompaniment to an oriental dinner.

4   oz. dry mustard
1   cup sugar
1   cup cider vinegar
¼   cup water
1   teaspoon salt
2   teaspoons dried dill weed
2   eggs, beaten

Combine all ingredients except eggs; let stand at room temperature at least 6 hours. Do not refrigerate. To prepare, stir eggs into mustard mixture in heavy saucepan; heat to boiling. Boil for 5 full minutes, stirring constantly. Cool and refrigerate until ready to serve. Serve with egg rolls or use as a dip for fresh vegetables.

Salads

Festive Romaine Salad

6 Servings

DRESSING

⅓ cup sugar
2 tablespoons poppy seeds
¾ cup mayonnaise
¼ cup milk
2 tablespoons vinegar

SALAD

1 bunch romaine lettuce or mixed greens, torn
½ red onion
Seeds of 1 pomegranate (or 1 pint fresh strawberries, sliced)

DRESSING: Combine all dressing ingredients in small bowl; mix well.
SALAD: Combine all salad ingredients in large bowl; toss with dressing.

Ernesta's Greek Salad

6 Servings

DRESSING

2 to 3 teaspoons garlic powder
2 to 3 teaspoons ground basil
2¼ teaspoons freshly ground black pepper
⅛ teaspoon salt
1 tablespoon snipped fresh tarragon
2 eggs
¼ cup Dijon mustard
2 tablespoons soy sauce
¼ cup red wine vinegar
Dash of hot pepper sauce
¾ cup vegetable oil

SALAD

2 cucumbers, peeled, seeded and chopped
½ red onion, thinly sliced
1 large head romaine lettuce, torn
2 tomatoes, sliced into thirds
6 oz. Feta cheese, crumbled
12 Greek olives

DRESSING: Combine all dressing ingredients in medium bowl; mix well. Refrigerate until serving time.
SALAD: Combine all salad ingredients in large bowl. Pour dressing over salad; toss gently.

Salad Elaine

6 to 8 Servings

Homemade croutons make a difference.

DRESSING

½ cup sugar
2 teaspoons celery seed
1 teaspoon dry mustard
1 teaspoon salt
3 tablespoons grated onion
⅓ cup vinegar
1 cup light vegetable oil (safflower)

SALAD

4 cups torn lettuce (romaine, red, iceberg)
1 cup halved red and green seedless grapes
1 large apple, chopped
½ cup chopped celery
½ cup chopped walnuts
⅓ cup crumbled Bleu cheese
½ cup Cheesy Herb Croutons (recipe below)

DRESSING: Combine all dressing ingredients in small bowl; mix well.
SALAD: Combine all salad ingredients in large bowl; toss with dressing. Top with croutons just before serving.

Cheesy Herb Croutons

3 to 5 Cups

½ loaf very thin-sliced white bread
3 tablespoons olive oil
½ cup grated Romano cheese
2 to 3 teaspoons garlic powder
1½ to 2 teaspoons dried salad herbs, crushed

Heat oven to 225°F. Cut bread into ½-inch cubes; place on cookie sheet. Sprinkle with olive oil. Combine cheese, garlic powder and herbs; sprinkle over bread. Bake at 225°F. for 1 hour. Cool; refrigerate tightly covered.

Gruyere Salad

8 to 10 Servings

A savory combination. Can be served as a main dish salad for lunch.

DRESSING

¼ cup white wine vinegar
2 tablespoons Dijon mustard
¼ teaspoon salt
   Freshly ground pepper to taste
⅔ cup olive oil

SALAD

8 oz. (2 cups) shredded Gruyere cheese
1 cup diced celery
1 cup diced green pepper
1 cup sliced ripe olives
1 cup sliced fresh mushrooms
½ cup sliced green onions

4 cups fresh spinach, cleaned and torn

DRESSING: Combine all dressing ingredients in small bowl; mix well.

SALAD: Combine cheese, celery, green pepper, olives, mushrooms and green onions in large bowl. Pour dressing over salad. Refrigerate 2 hours or overnight. Toss with spinach just before serving.

Germantown Coleslaw

8 to 10 Servings

Rosebud Grocery, Edina and Minnetonka, Joan Donatelle

Rosebud Grocery is a favorite deli-stop for hungry shoppers.

DRESSING

2 cups mayonnaise
1 tablespoon red wine vinegar
   Salt and freshly ground pepper

SALAD

1 small head green cabbage, chopped
1 small red onion, diced
1 carrot, shredded
8 oz. Cheddar cheese, cubed
8 oz. cooked ham, cubed
1 tablespoon snipped fresh parsley
1 green pepper, diced

DRESSING: Combine mayonnaise, vinegar and salt and pepper to taste in small bowl; mix well.

SALAD: Combine all salad ingredients in large bowl; toss with dressing. Serve chilled.

Spinach-Peanut Salad with Curry Dressing

8 Servings

The sweet chutney and tangy mustard are a unique taste combination.

DRESSING

⅓ cup vegetable oil
¼ cup white wine vinegar
2 teaspoons finely minced chutney
½ teaspoon curry powder
½ teaspoon salt
4 to 6 drops hot pepper sauce
½ teaspoon dry mustard

SALAD

1 lb. fresh spinach, cleaned and torn
2 tart apples, peeled and coarsely chopped
4 teaspoons fresh lemon juice
1 cup dry-roasted peanuts
½ cup sliced scallions

DRESSING: Combine all dressing ingredients in small bowl; mix well.
SALAD: Place spinach in large bowl. Toss apples in lemon juice; add apples, peanuts and scallions to spinach. Pour dressing over salad; toss.

Endive, Cabbage and Walnut Salad

8 Servings

Layer salad ingredients in a glass serving bowl for a beautiful presentation. Toss with dressing at the table.

DRESSING

2 small green onions, cut up
⅓ cup coarsely chopped fresh parsley
⅓ cup red wine vinegar
1 tablespoon Dijon mustard
½ teaspoon dried tarragon leaves, crumbled
Dash sugar
Salt and pepper
1 cup vegetable oil

SALAD

1 lb. curly endive, torn
1 cup chopped fresh parsley
¼ head red cabbage, sliced
1 cup chopped walnuts

DRESSING: Mince green onions and ⅓ cup parsley in food processor or blender. Add remaining dressing ingredients except oil. With processor running, gradually add oil. Refrigerate.
SALAD: Combine endive, 1 cup parsley, cabbage and walnuts in large bowl. Pour dressing over salad; toss.

Green Salad with Raspberry Vinaigrette

6 to 8 Servings

A festive red and green salad, perfect during the holidays.

¼ cup raspberry vinegar
2 tablespoons honey
½ teaspoon sugar
¼ teaspoon fresh lemon juice
¼ teaspoon salt
¼ cup vegetable oil
¼ cup olive oil

SALAD

4 to 5 cups torn mixed greens
½ pint fresh raspberries
1 medium green onion, sliced
½ cup chopped walnuts or pecans

DRESSING: Combine all dressing ingredients in small bowl; mix well.
SALAD: Combine all salad ingredients in large bowl; gently toss with dressing.

Feta and Walnut Spinach Salad with Basil Dressing

6 Servings

BASIL DRESSING

½ cup olive oil
¼ cup red wine vinegar
1 tablespoon dried basil leaves, crushed
2 teaspoons sugar
1 clove garlic, minced
Salt and pepper

SALAD

1 bunch fresh spinach, cleaned and torn
1 avocado, peeled and thinly sliced
½ red onion, thinly sliced
½ cup crumbled Feta cheese
½ cup coarsely chopped walnuts, toasted
Greek olives

DRESSING: Combine all dressing ingredients in blender container; mix well. Refrigerate. Shake well before using.
SALAD: Combine all salad ingredients except olives in large bowl. Pour dressing over salad; toss. Garnish with olives.

Spinach Salad with Chutney-Mustard Dressing

4 to 6 Servings

DRESSING

¼ cup wine vinegar
2 to 3 tablespoons chutney
1 clove garlic, minced
2 tablespoons Dijon mustard
2 teaspoons sugar
⅓ to ½ cup vegetable oil
   Salt and freshly ground pepper

SALAD

1 lb. fresh spinach leaves, cleaned and torn
8 oz. fresh mushrooms, sliced
1 cup sliced water chestnuts
½ lb. bacon, crisply fried and crumbled
¾ cup fresh bean sprouts
4 oz. (1 cup) shredded Gruyere or Swiss cheese
¼ cup thinly sliced red onion

DRESSING: Combine vinegar, chutney, garlic, mustard and sugar in blender or food processor. With machine running, add oil in a slow steady stream. Mix until thick and smooth; salt and pepper to taste. Refrigerate. Let stand at room temperature 30 minutes before serving.

SALAD: Combine all salad ingredients in large bowl. Pour dressing over salad; toss.

Summer Salad

6 Servings

3 medium tomatoes, peeled and sliced
1 green pepper, sliced into rings
1 medium onion, sliced
⅓ cup vegetable oil
1 teaspoon onion salt
¼ teaspoon sugar
⅛ teaspoon black pepper
1 teaspoon celery seed
1 tablespoon snipped fresh parsley
3 tablespoons lemon juice
1 tablespoon dry gin, if desired

Layer tomatoes, green pepper and onion in serving bowl. Combine remaining ingredients; mix thoroughly. Pour over layers. Refrigerate at least 1 hour before serving. Baste frequently with marinade.

California Salad

8 to 10 Servings

DRESSING

Juice of 1 lemon
3 cloves garlic, minced
Salt and pepper to taste
¾ cup olive oil

SALAD

¼ lb. bacon, diced
2 heads romaine lettuce
2 cups cherry tomatoes, halved
1 cup sliced fresh mushrooms
4 oz. (1 cup) shredded Swiss cheese
⅔ cup slivered almonds, toasted
⅓ cup grated Parmesan cheese
1 cup croutons, if desired
½ cup sliced ripe olives, if desired

DRESSING: Combine all dressing ingredients in large bowl; mix well.

SALAD: Fry bacon, drain on paper towels. Place remaining salad ingredients except croutons and olives in bowl with dressing; toss. Garnish with croutons and olives.

Mushroom and Avocado Salad

4 to 6 Servings

Avocados should be slightly firm to the touch when purchased. Allow to ripen at room temperature several days until soft.

DRESSING

¼ cup fresh lime juice
½ teaspoon salt
1 to 2 cloves garlic, minced
¾ teaspoon ground coriander
Freshly ground pepper
¼ cup vegetable oil
¼ cup olive oil

SALAD

8 oz. fresh mushrooms, sliced
2 ripe avocados, peeled and diced
2 green onions, sliced
Leaf or red lettuce

DRESSING: Combine all dressing ingredients in small bowl; mix well.

SALAD: Combine mushrooms, avocados and onions in refrigerator container. Pour dressing over vegetables. Cover; refrigerate at least 4 hours. Serve over leaf lettuce.

Viltoft Dressing

4 Cups

This dressing adds creamy goodness to any green salad.

Radisson Hotel South and Plaza Tower, Minneapolis, Tim Grenell

2   egg yolks
2   cups mayonnaise
¾   cup buttermilk
¾   cup grated Parmesan cheese
1½ cups vegetable oil
1   tablespoon dry mustard
2   teaspoons minced garlic
6   tablespoons tarragon vinegar
3   tablespoons lemon juice
1½ tablespoons Worcestershire sauce
3   tablespoons freshly cracked pepper
1   drop hot pepper sauce
    Dash salt

Whip egg yolks into mayonnaise in small bowl, with electric mixer. Blend in buttermilk and cheese. Increase mixer speed while slowly adding oil; blend until fully incorporated. Decrease mixer speed; blend in remaining ingredients.

Pepper Cream Dressing

About 5 Cups

Fitzgerald's, St. Paul, Tom Robertson

1   tablespoon sugar
1   tablespoon coarse salt
1⅛ teaspoons cracked pepper
¾   to 1 teaspoon garlic powder
2   tablespoons Maggi seasoning
¼   cup red wine vinegar
2   tablespoons lemon juice
¾   cup salad dressing
¾   cup mayonnaise
1½ teaspoons snipped fresh parsley
¼   cup minced onion
6   oz. (2 cups) grated Parmesan cheese
1   cup buttermilk

Combine sugar, salt, pepper and garlic powder with Maggi seasoning, vinegar and lemon juice. Whip salad dressing and mayonnaise in large bowl until smooth. Blend in sugar mixture and remaining ingredients. Refrigerate until ready to serve.

Cabbage Salad

8 to 10 Servings

DRESSING

2 cups mayonnaise
⅓ cup grated Parmesan cheese
½ cup sugar
2 cloves garlic, minced
   Juice of ½ lemon

SALAD

1 small to medium head cabbage, shredded
1 bunch broccoli, broken into florets
1 (10-oz.) pkg. frozen peas, thawed
8 oz. fresh mushrooms, sliced
2 cups chopped celery
1 bunch green onions, sliced
1 lb. bacon, fried and crumbled

DRESSING: Combine all dressing ingredients in small bowl; mix well.

SALAD: Combine all salad ingredients except bacon in large bowl; mix well. Add salad dressing and bacon; toss.

Cauliflower Salad

8 to 10 Servings

A hearty winter salad.

DRESSING

2 cups mayonnaise
¼ cup sugar
2 tablespoons vinegar

SALAD

1 head cauliflower, broken into florets
1 bunch broccoli, broken into florets
1 small onion, grated
8 oz. (2 cups) shredded Mozzarella cheese
¼ cup grated Parmesan cheese
1 lb. bacon, fried and crumbled

DRESSING: Combine all dressing ingredients; mix well.

SALAD: Combine vegetables, cheeses and bacon in large bowl. Add dressing to vegetable mixture; toss.

Oriental Stuffed Baguette

6 Servings

<u>DRESSING</u>

6   tablespoons vegetable oil
2   tablespoons sesame seeds
1   teaspoon ground ginger
3   tablespoons wine vinegar
1½ tablespoons soy sauce
1   teaspoon sugar
1   clove garlic, minced
⅓   cup sliced green onion

<u>SALAD</u>

½   lb. sliced cooked ham, cut into julienne strips
1   (8-oz.) can sliced water chestnuts, drained
1   (6-oz.) pkg. frozen Chinese pea pods, thawed and patted dry
8   oz. fresh mushrooms, thinly sliced

1   (1-lb.) loaf sourdough French bread

<u>DRESSING</u>: Combine oil and sesame seeds in skillet; heat over medium-low heat until seeds are golden, 2 to 4 minutes. Cool. Stir in remaining dressing ingredients.

<u>SALAD</u>: Combine all salad ingredients. Reserve 2 tablespoons dressing; combine remaining dressing with salad ingredients. Slice French bread in half lengthwise. Remove bread from inside of bottom slice, leaving a shell about ½ to 1-inch thick. To assemble loaf, spread reserved dressing on cut side of top half; fill shell with salad. Replace top. Bread can be filled up to 4 hours before serving. To serve, cut into thick slices or sections.

Curry Mayonnaise for Poultry

1½ Cups

Serve curry mayonnaise over cold poached chicken as a main course; garnish with parsley sprigs and/or chopped peanuts. Or serve with quartered hard-cooked eggs as a first course.

1 tablespoon olive oil
1 small onion, finely chopped
1 tablespoon curry powder
½ cup chicken stock
1 teaspoon tomato puree or paste
2 tablespoons apricot jam or sweet mango chutney
  Juice of ½ lemon, strained
1 cup mayonnaise
3 tablespoons whipping cream

Heat oil in saucepan. Saute onion 5 minutes until tender but not brown. Stir in curry powder; cook a few minutes to bring out flavors. Stir in stock and tomato puree. Add jam and lemon juice; stir until mixture boils. Reduce heat; simmer 5 minutes. Strain into bowl; refrigerate. Combine chilled mixture and mayonnaise; stir in cream just before using.

Roast Beef and Avocado Salad

8 Servings

DRESSING

½ cup vegetable oil
¼ cup olive oil
¼ cup red wine vinegar
2 teaspoons Dijon mustard
2 teaspoons salt
¼ teaspoon pepper

SALAD

2 lb. rare roast beef, thinly sliced
2 to 3 avocados, sliced
1 medium sweet onion, very thinly sliced
  Bibb or green leaf lettuce

DRESSING: Combine all dressing ingredients in small bowl; mix well.
SALAD: Cut beef into ½-inch wide pieces. Layer beef, avocados and onion in bowl. Pour dressing over layers. Cover; refrigerate several hours or overnight. Serve on lettuce.

TIP: *Use deli roast beef or plan ahead and prepare extra when you grill or roast beef.*

Chicken Waldorf Salad

6 Servings

*St. James Hotel, Red Wing,
Charles Worth*

*The St. James Hotel is a
restored hotel located in Red
Wing, Minnesota.*

DRESSING

1½ cups mayonnaise
1   tablespoon sugar
1   tablespoon lemon juice

SALAD

2   stalks celery, finely diced
6   red apples, diced
1   small head iceberg lettuce, torn
½   cup shredded red cabbage
1   carrot, thinly sliced
6   (4-oz.) boneless chicken breasts (poached in white wine and chicken
       stock), each cut into 8 strips
6   tablespoons chopped walnuts, toasted
18 leaf lettuce leaves
18 fresh strawberries
12 slices kiwifruit
6   small bunches grapes

DRESSING: Combine all dressing ingredients in medium bowl; mix well.
    SALAD: Fold celery and apples into dressing. Toss iceberg lettuce with
cabbage and carrot in separate bowl. Place 3 lettuce leaves on individual
salad plate; top with ⅙ of lettuce mixture and ⅙ of apple mixture. Repeat
with remaining lettuce leaves and salad mixtures. Top each plate with 8
chicken strips; sprinkle with walnuts. Garnish with strawberries, kiwi and
grapes.

Red Wine Vinaigrette

1¼ Cups

1   teaspoon salt
½   teaspoon dry mustard
½   teaspoon dried oregano leaves, crushed
¼   teaspoon pepper
¼   teaspoon cayenne pepper
1   clove garlic, minced
¼   cup red wine vinegar
    Dash hot pepper sauce
1   cup vegetable oil

Combine all ingredients in small bowl; mix well.

North Shore Chicken Salad

6 Servings

A spectacular salad featuring Minnesota wild rice. Great use for leftover chicken or turkey.

DRESSING

2 large cloves garlic, minced
1 tablespoon Dijon mustard
½ teaspoon salt
¼ teaspoon sugar
¼ teaspoon freshly ground pepper
¼ cup rice wine vinegar
⅓ cup vegetable oil

SALAD

4 cups cooked wild rice (cooked in chicken stock)
  Juice of ½ lemon
1 whole chicken breast, cooked and cubed
3 green onions, including tops, sliced
½ red pepper, diced
2 oz. pea pods, cut into 1-inch pieces
1 to 2 ripe avocados, cut into medium-size pieces
1 cup toasted pecan halves
  Lettuce leaves

DRESSING: Combine all dressing ingredients in food processor; blend thoroughly. (Or mix all ingredients together well in bowl.)

SALAD: Toss warm rice with lemon juice in medium bowl; cool. Add chicken, onions, red pepper and pea pods; toss with dressing. Cover; refrigerate 2 to 4 hours. Just before serving add avocado and pecans; toss gently. Transfer to salad bowl; garnish with lettuce leaves.

Caesar Salad

8 Servings

A favorite combination.

3 cloves garlic
3 anchovies
4 dashes Worcestershire sauce
3 tablespoons white wine vinegar
3 tablespoons lemon juice
½ cup olive oil
½ cup grated Parmesan cheese
1 tablespoon Dijon mustard
3 hard-cooked eggs, finely chopped
1 head romaine lettuce, torn
1 cup garlic and cheese croutons
  Freshly ground pepper

Crush garlic and mash anchovies in wooden salad bowl. Stir in Worcestershire sauce, vinegar, lemon juice and oil. Blend in cheese, mustard and eggs; mix well. Let dressing stand 30 to 60 minutes to blend flavors. Toss with romaine, croutons and pepper to taste.

TIP: *A recipe for Cheesy-Herb croutons can be found on page 77.*

Grapefruit-Avocado Salad with Poppy Seed Dressing

8 to 10 Servings

Salad can be arranged in layers in glass bowl. Pour dressing over salad; toss just before serving.

DRESSING

¾ cup sugar
⅓ cup vinegar
1 teaspoon dry mustard
1 teaspoon salt
1½ tablespoons grated onion
1 cup vegetable oil
1½ tablespoons poppy seeds

SALAD

4 heads bibb lettuce, torn
2 avocados, peeled and cut into medium-size pieces
2 grapefruit, sectioned and cut into medium-size pieces
1 pint fresh strawberries, halved

DRESSING: Combine sugar, vinegar, mustard, salt and onion in blender or food processor. With processor running, add oil very slowly until well mixed. Just before serving stir in poppy seeds.

SALAD: Combine all salad ingredients in large bowl. Pour dressing over salad; toss.

Curried Chicken Tomato Cups

4 Servings

2 whole chicken breasts, skinned and boned
2 tablespoons vegetable oil
1 medium onion, chopped
1 teaspoon curry powder
½ teaspoon salt
½ cup mayonnaise
1 tablespoon lemon juice
1 celery stalk, sliced
4 ripe tomatoes
  Lettuce leaves
  Seedless grapes, halved

Cut chicken into ¼-inch slices; set aside. Heat oil in skillet over high heat; sauté onion until tender. Stir in chicken, curry powder and salt. Cook about 5 minutes or until chicken is tender, stirring frequently; cool. Combine cooked chicken and onion with mayonnaise, lemon juice and celery in large bowl; mix well. Refrigerate. Cut each tomato into 6 to 8 wedges, cutting to, but not through, base of tomato. To serve: Place tomatoes on lettuce-lined plates. Spread wedges slightly apart; fill with chicken mixture. Garnish with grapes.

Steering Committee Luncheon Shrimp Salad

8 Servings

This recipe originated at one of our many Cookbook Steering Committee meetings.

DRESSING

¼ cup white wine vinegar
2 tablespoons lemon juice
½ teaspoon dry mustard
½ teaspoon freshly ground pepper
¼ teaspoon salt
1 clove garlic, minced
½ small onion, finely chopped
¾ cup vegetable oil

SALAD

16 extra large shrimp, cooked, peeled and deveined
1 bunch spinach, cleaned and torn
1 head red leaf lettuce, torn
1 red bell pepper, sliced into ¼-inch strips
1 bunch green onions, coarsely chopped
4 celery stalks, coarsely chopped
1 cucumber, peeled, seeded and chopped
4 carrots, diced
½ turnip, cut into ½-inch strips
8 oz. (1 cup) Swiss cheese, shredded
1 (8½-oz.) can artichoke hearts, cut into quarters
1 (8½-oz.) can hearts of palm, sliced into ¼-inch strips
4 hard-cooked eggs, sliced

DRESSING: Combine all dressing ingredients in small bowl; mix well.

SALAD: Combine all ingredients in large bowl; pour dressing over salad. Serve immediately.

North Country Potato Salad

12 Servings

A potato salad with no mayonnaise to serve on a summer picnic.

SALAD

1 lb. bacon, cut into 1-inch pieces
3 lb. new potatoes
1 lb. fresh green beans

DRESSING

½ cup thinly sliced green onion
¼ cup snipped fresh parsley
1 teaspoon salt
1 teaspoon dry mustard
½ teaspoon dried basil leaves, crushed
½ teaspoon dried tarragon leaves, crushed
Freshly ground black pepper
1 clove garlic, minced
¼ cup tarragon vinegar
¼ cup consomme or chicken broth
½ cup vegetable oil

SALAD: Fry bacon until crisp; drain on paper towels. Slice potatoes into ¼-inch slices; cook in boiling water about 15 minutes or until tender but not soft; drain. Cut green beans into 2-inch lengths. Cook until tender-crisp, about 8 minutes. Place potatoes and beans in large bowl.
DRESSING: Combine all dressing ingredients in small bowl; mix well. Pour over warm vegetables; add bacon and toss gently. Serve at room temperature.

Dayton's Marketplace Smoked Turkey Jarlsberg

6 to 8 Servings

A specialty at Dayton's Marketplace, located at 700 Under the Mall downtown in Dayton's department store.

1½ cups mayonnaise
3 to 4 tablespoons raspberry vinegar
1 tablespoon crushed green peppercorns
1½ lb. smoked turkey breast, cut into julienne strips
¾ lb. Jarlsberg cheese, cut into julienne strips
¾ lb. whole red seedless grapes
1 stalk celery, chopped

TIP: *Salad can be made 24 hours ahead and refrigerated.*

Combine mayonnaise, vinegar and peppercorns in large bowl; mix well. Add remaining ingredients; toss.

Raw Vegetable Salad

8 to 10 Servings

This salad is a favorite of Tommy Kramer, Quarterback, Minnesota Vikings.

2   cups cauliflower florets
2   cups broccoli florets
4   green onions, including tops, sliced
1   (10-oz.) pkg. frozen peas (or 1 (16-oz.) can peas, drained)

DRESSING

1   cup dairy sour cream
½   cup mayonnaise
½   to ¾ teaspoon garlic powder
½   teaspoon salt
½   teaspoon pepper

Combine vegetables in large bowl.
    DRESSING: Combine all dressing ingredients in small bowl; mix well. Pour over vegetables and toss. Refrigerate several hours or overnight.

Snow Pea, Mushroom and Red Pepper Salad

8 Servings

An interesting blend of shapes and colors.

1   (7-oz.) pkg. frozen pea pods (or 4 oz. fresh pea pods)
⅓   cup vegetable oil
2   tablespoons white wine vinegar
1   tablespoon lemon juice
1   clove garlic, minced
1   tablespoon sugar
½   teaspoon salt
1   red bell pepper, cut into ¼-inch strips, lengthwise
8   oz. fresh mushrooms, sliced
2   tablespoons sesame seeds, toasted

TIP: *If fresh pea pods are used, cook 5 minutes.*

Cook pea pods according to package directions; drain and refrigerate. Combine oil, vinegar, lemon juice, garlic, sugar and salt in medium bowl; mix well. Add pea pods, red pepper and mushrooms; toss until vegetables are well coated with dressing. Refrigerate to chill. Before serving, arrange vegetables on individual salad plates; sprinkle with sesame seeds.

Soups

Green Gazpacho

8 Servings

A perfect accompaniment to grilled meats and seafood. A new version of gazpacho with no tomatoes.

2   cloves garlic, quartered
4   shallots, quartered
2   green peppers, coarsely chopped
2   cucumbers, peeled, seeded and chopped
2   cups watercress
2   tablespoons chopped fresh dill (or 2 teaspoons dried dill weed)
2   (14-oz.) cans chicken broth
8   teaspoons red wine vinegar
1   cup mayonnaise
1   cup dairy sour cream
    Salt and pepper
    Thinly sliced cucumbers

Combine garlic, shallots, green peppers, chopped cucumbers, watercress, dill, chicken broth and vinegar in blender; blend 5 minutes or until very smooth. (Food processor does not work well.) Pour into large bowl. Whisk mayonnaise and sour cream together; whisk into soup. Salt and pepper to taste. Refrigerate several hours or overnight. Garnish with thin cucumber slices.

Carrot-Ginger Soup

6 Servings

Duggan's Bar and Grill, St. Louis Park, Dave Ariz

Duggan's restaurant serves elegant food in a casual setting.

6   tablespoons unsalted butter
1   medium onion, chopped
4   cloves garlic, minced
¼   cup peeled, chopped fresh gingerroot
1   cup white wine
7   cups chicken broth
2   tablespoons fresh lemon juice
1½   lb. carrots, shredded
     Dash curry powder
     Salt and pepper to taste
1   tablespoon honey, if desired
     Snipped fresh chives or parsley

TIP: *Leftover fresh gingerroot can be frozen. It's texture changes but its pungent flavor will remain.*

Melt butter in large saucepan. Saute onion, garlic and ginger 15 minutes (do not brown). Stir in wine, broth, lemon juice and carrots; simmer 45 minutes. Remove from heat; puree in blender. Add curry powder, salt, pepper and honey. Serve hot or cold. Garnish with chives or parsley.

Carrot Soup

4 Servings

Also serve with French Colombard wine as a beverage because the flavor is so distinctive.

1   cup chopped onion
2   tablespoons butter or margarine
2   cups sliced carrots
1½ cups chicken broth
¾   cup French Colombard wine
½   teaspoon dried dill weed
¼   teaspoon dried thyme leaves, crushed
    Salt and pepper
1   cup half-and-half
    Fresh parsley sprigs

Saute onion in butter; add carrots and broth. Simmer covered 20 minutes, stirring occasionally. Stir in wine and seasonings; reduce heat to evaporate the alcohol. Puree in blender or food processor; blend in half-and-half. Serve hot or cold; garnish with parsley.

Cucumber Soup

8 to 10 Servings

Serve this soup in the summer with fresh garden cucumbers.

3   cucumbers, peeled, seeded and shredded
1   onion, minced
3   scallions, minced
2   tablespoons butter or margarine
3   cups chicken broth
    Salt and white pepper
    Lemon juice to taste
1   cup dairy sour cream
    Snipped fresh chives

Drain cucumbers; reserve liquid. Saute cucumbers, onion and scallions in butter until soft but not brown. Combine cucumber mixture, reserved cucumber liquid, broth, salt and pepper in large saucepan. Simmer covered 20 minutes. Cool 20 minutes; stir in lemon juice. Puree in food processor or blender. Blend in sour cream with whisk. Refrigerate until chilled. Garnish with chives.

Cold Watermelon Soup

8 Servings

A pretty summer cooler; serve in clear glass bowls or punch cups.

TIP: *Do not make more than 4 hours ahead of serving to preserve fresh sweet flavor of soup.*

1   (5-lb.) watermelon
1   to 1¼ cups sugar (sweeten to taste)
2   cups red wine (Spanish sangria)
    Juice of ½ lemon
½   lemon, thinly sliced

Carefully remove seedless center of melon; cut into ¾-inch cubes. Sprinkle with 2 or 3 tablespoons sugar; cover and refrigerate. Remove seeds from remaining melon; puree melon in food processor or blender. Combine melon juice with wine; stir in remaining sugar, lemon juice and melon cubes. Refrigerate at least 3 hours. Serve chilled in bowls or glasses, garnish each serving with ½ slice lemon.

Hot and Sour Soup

5 Servings
(about 1 cup each)

Leeann Chin, Chinese Cuisine,
Minneapolis, Leeann Chin

6   medium dried black mushrooms
¼   lb. boneless pork loin
½   teaspoon cornstarch
½   teaspoon salt
½   teaspoon soy sauce (light or dark)
4   to 6 ounces bean curd (tofu)
4   cups chicken broth
3   tablespoons white vinegar
1   tablespoon soy sauce (light or dark)
1   teaspoon salt
½   cup shredded canned bamboo shoots
2   tablespoons cornstarch
2   tablespoons cold water
¼   teaspoon white pepper
2   eggs, slightly beaten
2   tablespoons chopped green onions, with tops
2   teaspoons red pepper sauce
½   teaspoon sesame oil

Soak mushrooms in warm water until soft, about 30 minutes; drain. Rinse in warm water; drain. Remove and discard stems; cut caps into thin slices. Trim fat from pork; shred pork. Toss pork, ½ teaspoon cornstarch, ½ teaspoon salt and ½ teaspoon soy sauce in glass or plastic bowl. Refrigerate, covered, 15 minutes. Cut bean curd into 1 x ½ x ¼-inch pieces. Heat chicken broth, vinegar, 1 tablespoon soy sauce and 1 teaspoon salt to boiling in 3-quart saucepan. Stir in bamboo shoots, mushrooms, pork and bean curd. Heat to boiling; reduce heat. Simmer, covered, 5 minutes. Mix 2 tablespoons cornstarch, the water and white pepper; stir into soup. Heat to boiling, stirring constantly. Pour egg slowly into soup, stirring constantly with fork until egg forms shreds. Stir in green onions, pepper sauce and sesame oil.

Pumpkin Soup with Wild Rice

8 Servings

Ann Burckhardt, TASTE Editor, Minneapolis Star Tribune

Wonderful year round as a first course with chicken or seafood.

TIP: *Two cups cooked buttercup or butternut squash can be substituted for pumpkin.*

1   cup chopped onion
2   tablespoons butter or margarine
4   cups chicken broth
1   (16-oz.) can pumpkin
1⅓ cups cooked wild rice
⅛   teaspoon white pepper
1   cup whipping cream
    Snipped fresh chives or parsley

Saute onion in butter in large saucepan. Stir in broth and pumpkin. Heat, stirring occasionally, over low heat 10 to 15 minutes. Stir in wild rice and pepper. Continue to heat 10 minutes. Stir in cream; heat through (do not boil). Garnish with chives or parsley; serve immediately.

Fresh Mushroom Soup

6 Servings

1   onion, finely sliced
1   clove garlic, minced
3   to 4 tablespoons butter or margarine
3   to 4 tablespoons vegetable oil
1   lb. fresh mushrooms, sliced
    Salt and pepper to taste
3   tablespoons tomato paste
¼   cup dry vermouth
3   cups chicken broth
3   egg yolks, beaten
2   tablespoons snipped fresh parsley
1   cup grated Parmesan cheese

Saute onion and garlic in butter and oil until soft but not brown. Stir in mushrooms; cook a few minutes. Stir in salt and pepper, tomato paste and vermouth; cook a few minutes longer. Stir in chicken broth; simmer about 15 minutes. Just before serving, stir in beaten egg yolks (do not boil); stir in cheese and parsley.

Cream of Spinach and Clam Soup

6 to 8 Servings

½   medium onion, diced
4   slices bacon
4   anchovy fillets, minced
1   clove garlic, minced
½   cup butter or margarine
2   tablespoons flour
4   cups chicken broth
1   (10½-oz.) pkg. frozen spinach, thawed
2   (6½-oz.) cans clams, drained
1   cup whipping cream
    Salt and freshly ground pepper
    Pernod, if desired

Lightly saute onion, bacon, anchovies and garlic in skillet over medium-high heat; remove from heat. Melt butter in large saucepan over medium-high heat. Blend in flour; cook 2 to 3 minutes, stirring constantly. Gradually stir in broth; heat to boiling, stirring constantly. Stir in bacon mixture, spinach and clams; heat to boiling, stirring occasionally. Stir in cream; heat to boiling. Salt and pepper to taste. Add dash of Pernod to each serving, if desired.

Scott Lake Minestrone

12 to 16 Servings

½ lb. bacon, chopped
½ lb. ham, chopped
½ lb. Italian sausage, sliced
4 to 6 cloves garlic, minced
1 small onion, chopped
6 quarts beef stock
1 (15-oz.) can kidney beans, undrained
3 cups shredded cabbage
1 cup diced celery
1 leek, chopped
2 medium zucchini, sliced
1½ cups red wine
1 teaspoon salt
1 teaspoon pepper
½ teaspoon ground allspice
1 (28-oz.) can Italian tomatoes, undrained
¼ cup snipped fresh basil (or 1 tablespoon dried)
1 cup uncooked elbow macaroni

Lightly brown bacon, ham, sausage, garlic and onion in Dutch oven or large skillet; drain. Heat stock in large saucepan; add bacon mixture, beans, cabbage, celery, leek, zucchini, wine, salt, pepper and allspice. Simmer 45 minutes. Stir in tomatoes, basil and macaroni; simmer about 15 minutes or until macaroni is tender.

Zuppa Di Funghi

6 to 8 Servings

2 slices bacon, minced
1 tablespoon snipped fresh parsley
1 lb. fresh mushrooms, thinly sliced
2½ tablespoons butter or margarine
6 cups chicken broth
1 egg, beaten
¼ cup grated Parmesan cheese
Salt and pepper

Fry bacon until crisp; remove from skillet and drain on paper towels. Saute parsley and mushrooms in butter about 5 minutes. Heat broth to boiling in large saucepan. Stir in mushroom mixture; simmer 15 minutes. Place egg and cheese in soup tureen; blend. Add soup and bacon; season to taste.

Lentil Soup with Hot Italian Sausage

4 Servings

Pronto Ristorante, Minneapolis, Mark Donnay

Fresh herbs enhance the flavor of this soup.

1½ cups dried lentils
½ cup finely diced carrots
½ cup finely diced celery
½ cup finely diced onion
    Olive oil
8 cups veal or beef bouillon
1 lb. hot Italian sausage, thinly sliced, cooked
    Fresh sage to taste
    Fresh basil to taste
    Salt and white pepper to taste

Rinse and sort lentils. Saute vegetables in small amount of olive oil until onions are transparent. Add lentils and bouillon. Simmer about 45 minutes or until lentils are tender. Add sausage, fresh herbs and salt and pepper to taste.

Dijon Sausage Soup

6 Servings

¼ lb. sweet Italian sausage, cooked, drained and crumbled
¼ lb. hot Italian sausage, cooked, drained and crumbled
2 (14-oz.) cans chicken broth
1 (16-oz.) can whole tomatoes, crushed
1 cup water
¾ cup uncooked brown rice
1 large onion, finely chopped
1 small carrot, finely chopped
1 to 2 large cloves garlic, minced
1 bay leaf
¼ teaspoon dried oregano leaves, crushed
¼ teaspoon dried basil leaves, crushed
½ cup rough Dijon mustard

Combine all ingredients except mustard in large saucepan. Simmer, covered, over medium heat 1 to 1½ hours or until rice is tender. Remove bay leaf, stir in mustard and serve.

Wild Rice Soup

8 to 10 Servings

*The Orion Room,
Minneapolis, Charles
Venables*

*The Orion Room is located on
the 50th floor of the IDS
building with spectacular
views of Minneapolis.*

STOCK

2	chicken carcasses
1	smoked ham bone
1	medium onion, sliced
	Salt and pepper to taste
1	bay leaf
¼	stalk celery, chopped
5	cups water
2	carrots, chopped

SOUP

2	cups cooked wild rice
2	tablespoons sliced blanched almonds
½	cup finely diced onion
½	cup finely diced celery
½	cup finely diced carrots
1	teaspoon red wine vinegar
¼	cup butter or margarine
2	teaspoons cornstarch, if desired
2	cups whipping cream

STOCK: Combine all stock ingredients in large stock pot; heat to boiling.
Simmer about 1½ hours. Strain and reserve for soup.

SOUP: Saute wild rice, almonds, onion, celery, carrots and vinegar in
butter in large saucepan. Stir in reserved soup stock; simmer about 1¼
hours. If necessary, thicken with cornstarch dissolved in small amount of
cream. Stir in remaining cream just before serving.

Tomato and Chive Soup

8 Servings

2 tablespoons butter or margarine
2 onions, chopped
2 carrots, chopped
2 leeks, chopped
2 cloves garlic, minced
½ teaspoon curry powder
¼ cup flour
2 (6-oz.) cans tomato paste
4 cups chicken broth
3 cups tomato juice
½ cup dry white wine
  Salt and pepper
½ cup dairy sour cream
2 tomatoes, chopped
¼ cup snipped fresh chives

Melt butter in heavy saucepan. Saute onions, carrots, leeks, garlic and curry powder over medium heat until vegetables are soft but not brown. Stir in flour and tomato paste. Immediately reduce heat; stir in chicken broth, tomato juice, wine, salt and pepper to taste. Simmer slowly 1 hour. Strain soup, if desired. Before serving garnish with sour cream, tomatoes and chives.

Fresh Tomato Bisque

6 Servings

Features the incomparable taste of Minnesota home-grown tomatoes.

1 medium onion, thinly sliced
1 tablespoon butter or margarine
2 lb. (about 6 medium) tomatoes, peeled, seeded and chopped
1½ tablespoons brown sugar
2 teaspoons finely chopped fresh basil
1 teaspoon salt
½ teaspoon pepper
2 whole cloves
1 bay leaf
2 cups half-and-half
1 cup milk
2 tablespoons snipped fresh chives or dill
6 large croutons

Saute onion in butter in large saucepan. Stir in tomatoes, brown sugar and seasonings. Simmer about 25 minutes, stirring occasionally. Remove cloves and bay leaf. Puree soup in blender; return to saucepan. Stir in half-and-half and milk; heat thoroughly. Garnish with chives and croutons.

Cream of Beet Soup

10 to 12 Servings

*Don't be misled by the title —
this is a unique and tasty
soup.*

6 medium beets, sliced (reserve beet greens)
½ head cabbage, shredded
2 stalks celery, chopped
2 carrots, chopped
3 medium onions, chopped
¼ cup butter or margarine
3 quarts chicken broth
½ teaspoon nutmeg
1 cup red wine
2 cups whipping cream
   Salt and pepper
   Whipped cream

Saute vegetables in butter in large saucepan 5 minutes. Add chicken broth;
simmer 20 to 30 minutes or until vegetables are tender. Stir in nutmeg and
wine; simmer 10 minutes. Puree mixture in blender or food processor;
return to saucepan. Stir in 2 cups cream; salt and pepper to taste. Serve at
room temperature or chilled. Garnish with whipped cream; sprinkle with
chopped reserved beet greens.

Cream of Asparagus Soup

6 Servings

2½ lb. fresh asparagus, peeled
4   cups water
¼   cup finely chopped onion
¼   cup snipped fresh parsley
1½ teaspoons snipped fresh coriander
3   tablespoons butter or margarine
2   tablespoons flour
1   chicken-flavor bouillon cube
½   cup whipping cream
2   tablespoons lemon juice
    Salt and pepper to taste
    Lemon slices

*TIP: If using thick asparagus,
peel the woody stems.*

Cook asparagus in 4 cups water 10 to 12 minutes or until very tender.
Remove asparagus from liquid; reserve 3 cups liquid. Cut off asparagus tips;
reserve. Cut remaining asparagus into 1-inch pieces. Saute onion, parsley
and coriander in butter in large saucepan until onion is tender. Stir in flour;
cook and stir 1 minute. Add bouillon cube and 3 cups asparagus liquid.
Simmer 5 minutes. Add 1-inch pieces of asparagus; puree mixture in
blender. Return to saucepan; stir in cream, lemon juice, salt, pepper and
reserved asparagus tips. Heat thoroughly; garnish with lemon slices.

Chili Con Carne

6 Servings

Mary Hart, Minneapolis Star Tribune.

Mary Hart is a long-time food writer for the Minneapolis Star Tribune.

1 lb. ground beef
1 large onion, sliced
½ cup chopped green pepper
3 cups cooked or canned tomatoes
1½ teaspoons salt
⅛ teaspoon paprika
⅛ teaspoon pepper
   Several whole cloves
1 bay leaf
1 teaspoon sugar
2 tablespoons chili powder
1 (15-oz.) can kidney beans

Brown ground beef, onion and green pepper together; drain. Stir in tomatoes and seasonings; simmer about 2 hours. (Add water and more tomatoes if needed.) Stir in beans; heat thoroughly.

Onion Wine Soup

6 to 8 Servings

Nancy Reagan submitted this recipe from the White House.

¼ cup butter
5 large onions, chopped
5 cups beef broth
½ cup celery leaves
1 large potato, sliced
1 cup dry white wine
1 tablespoon vinegar
2 teaspoons sugar
1 cup half-and-half
1 tablespoon snipped fresh parsley
   Salt and pepper

Melt butter in large saucepan. Add chopped onion and mix well. Add beef broth, celery leaves and potato; heat to boiling. Reduce heat; simmer covered 30 minutes. Puree mixture in blender. Return to saucepan and blend in wine, vinegar and sugar. Heat to boiling; reduce heat and simmer 5 minutes. Stir in half-and-half, parsley and salt and pepper to taste. Heat thoroughly; do not boil.

Breads

Treasure Toffee Coffee Cake

1 Coffee Cake

COFFEE CAKE

2   cups all-purpose flour
1½ teaspoons baking powder
1   teaspoon baking soda
¼   teaspoon salt
⅓   cup butter or margarine, softened
1   cup sugar
2   eggs
1   cup dairy sour cream
1   teaspoon vanilla

TOPPING

¼   cup sugar
1   teaspoon cinnamon
¼   cup chopped walnuts
¼   cup butter or margarine, melted
3   (1⅛-oz.) Heath candy bars, crushed

COFFEE CAKE: Heat oven to 325 °F. Grease 12-cup fluted tube pan. Combine flour, baking powder, soda and salt in large bowl; set aside. Cream butter and 1 cup sugar in separate bowl; add eggs and beat well. Blend in sour cream and vanilla. Blend in flour mixture. Pour ⅓ of batter into prepared pan.

TOPPING: Combine ¼ cup sugar, cinnamon, nuts and melted butter; sprinkle half of mixture over batter. Spoon ⅓ of batter over cinnamon mixture. Sprinkle crushed candy over batter. Spoon in remaining batter; top with remaining cinnamon mixture. Bake at 325 °F. for 40 to 45 minutes or until toothpick inserted in center comes out clean. Cool 10 minutes in pan. Invert onto rack to cool completely.

TIP: *Freeze Heath bars for easier crushing.*

Swedish Pancakes

25 (2-inch) Pancakes

Serve with lingonberries, a Swedish favorite.

6   eggs
⅓   cup sugar
1   tablespoon butter or margarine, melted
2   cups half-and-half
1   cup all-purpose flour
    Dash salt

Combine eggs and sugar in blender or food processor; blend slowly. With motor running, add butter and half-and-half; gradually add flour and salt. Batter will be very thin. Fry 2-inch pancakes on griddle or in skillet at 350 °F. to 375 °F.

Pineapple Cream Cheese Coffee Cake

1 Coffee Cake

<u>COFFEE CAKE</u>

1   (3-oz.) pkg. cream cheese, softened
2   tablespoons sugar
¼   teaspoon almond extract
1   (8¼-oz.) can crushed pineapple, drained (reserve juice)
¼   cup butter or margarine
½   cup sugar
1   egg
1   teaspoon vanilla
1¼   cups all-purpose flour
1½   teaspoons baking powder
¼   teaspoon salt

<u>TOPPING</u>

¼   cup packed brown sugar
2   tablespoons flour
2   tablespoons butter or margarine, softened
¼   cup flaked coconut
¼   teaspoon cinnamon
¼   cup sliced almonds

Heat oven to 350°F. Grease 8-inch square pan. Combine cream cheese, 2 tablespoons sugar, almond extract and 2 tablespoons pineapple; set aside. Cream butter and ½ cup sugar. Add egg and vanilla; beat until mixture is light and fluffy. Combine flour, baking powder and salt. Measure reserved juice; add water to make ½ cup liquid. Blend dry ingredients and pineapple liquid alternately into creamed mixture. Spread ½ of batter in prepared pan; top with crushed pineapple. Add remaining batter. Spoon cream cheese mixture, ½ teaspoon at a time, on top of cake.

<u>TOPPING:</u> Combine all topping ingredients in small bowl. Sprinkle over cream cheese mixture. Bake on center oven rack at 350°F. for 35 to 40 minutes or until toothpick inserted in center comes out clean.

Pumpkin Muffins

3 to 4 Dozen

3 cups sugar
1 cup butter or margarine, softened
3 eggs
1 (16-oz.) can pumpkin
1 teaspoon vanilla
3 cups all-purpose flour
1 teaspoon baking soda
1 teaspoon ground cloves
1 teaspoon nutmeg
1 teaspoon cinnamon
½ teaspoon baking powder
¼ teaspoon salt
¾ cup raisins
¾ cup chopped dates

Heat oven to 350°F. Grease muffin cups or line with paper baking cups. Cream sugar and butter in large bowl; stir in eggs, pumpkin and vanilla. Combine dry ingredients; stir into pumpkin mixture just until moistened. Fold in raisins and dates. Fill prepared muffin cups about ⅔ full. Bake at 350°F. for 25 to 30 minutes or until toothpick inserted in center comes out clean. Remove from pans.

Rhubarb Muffins

1½ Dozen

1½ cups packed brown sugar
⅔ cup vegetable oil
1 cup buttermilk
1 egg, slightly beaten
1 teaspoon vanilla
2½ cups all-purpose flour
1 teaspoon baking soda
1 teaspoon salt
1½ cups diced rhubarb
½ cup packed brown sugar
1 teaspoon margarine, melted

Heat oven to 325°F. Grease muffin cups or line with paper baking cups. Combine 1½ cups brown sugar, oil, buttermilk, egg and vanilla. Combine flour, soda and salt; blend into liquid mixture, stirring just until flour is moistened. Fold in rhubarb. Fill prepared muffin cups ¾ full. Combine remaining brown sugar with margarine; sprinkle on tops of muffins. Bake at 325°F. for 35 minutes or until toothpick inserted in center comes out clean. Remove from pans.

Strawberry Bread with Strawberry Butter

2 (9 x 5-inch)
or 5 Mini Loaves

BREAD

3   cups all-purpose flour
2   cups sugar
1   teaspoon baking soda
1   teaspoon salt
1   teaspoon cinnamon
4   eggs, beaten
¼   cup vegetable oil
2   (10-oz.) pkg. frozen strawberries, drained (reserve juice)

BUTTER

½   cup butter or margarine
½   cup reserved strawberry juice
½   to 1 cup powdered sugar

Heat oven to 350 °F. Grease and flour 2 (9 x 5-inch) or 5 mini loaf pans.
Combine dry ingredients in large bowl; make a well in center. Stir in eggs,
oil and strawberries; mix well. (If batter is not of medium consistency add
some of reserved strawberry juice.) Pour into prepared loaf pans. Bake at
350 °F. for 50 to 60 minutes or until toothpick inserted in center comes out
clean. (Bake mini loaf pans 20 to 25 minutes.) Cool 10 minutes in pans.
Remove from pans; cool completely on rack.
  BUTTER: Cream butter or margarine. Add powdered sugar and enough
of the reserved juice to make a creamy mixture; refrigerate.

Everybody's Favorite Bran Muffins

2 Dozen

7   oz. (3½ cups) raisin bran cereal
1½   cups sugar
2½   cups all-purpose flour
2½   teaspoons baking soda
1   teaspoon salt
1   teaspoon cinnamon
2   eggs
¼   cup butter or margarine, melted
¼   cup vegetable oil
2   cups buttermilk

TIP: *Batter can be*
refrigerated in a tightly
covered container 2 to 3
weeks.

Combine dry ingredients in large bowl. Whisk eggs, butter, oil and buttermilk together. Add egg mixture to dry mixture, mixing well. Refrigerate,
covered, 1 hour or longer. Heat oven to 350 °F. Grease muffin cups or line
with paper baking cups. Fill prepared muffin cups ⅔ full. Bake at 350 °F. for
about 20 minutes or until toothpick inserted in center comes out clean.
Remove from pans.

Apricot Bread

1 (8 x 4-inch) Loaf

Makes a quick and easy hostess gift.

1 (6-oz.) pkg. dried apricots, diced
1 cup sugar
½ teaspoon salt
½ teaspoon cinnamon
½ teaspoon ground cloves
¼ teaspoon nutmeg
1 cup water
6 tablespoons shortening
1 egg, beaten
2 cups all-purpose flour
1 teaspoon baking soda
½ cup chopped nuts, if desired

TIP: *Diced dried apples can be substituted for dried apricots.*

Heat oven to 350°F. Line 8 x 4-inch loaf pan with foil. Cook apricots, sugar, spices and water in saucepan over medium heat 5 minutes. Stir in shortening; cool completely. Blend in egg. Combine flour and soda; add to fruit mixture and mix well. Stir in nuts. Bake at 350°F. for 50 to 60 minutes or until toothpick inserted in center comes out clean. Cool 10 minutes in pan. Remove to rack to cool completely.

Swedish Rye Bread Supreme

2 (8 x 4-inch) Loaves

A traditional favorite. Great for making turkey sandwiches.

¼ cup packed brown sugar
¼ cup light molasses
1 tablespoon salt
2 tablespoons shortening
1½ cups boiling water
1 pkg. active dry yeast
¼ cup warm water (105°F. to 115°F.)
2½ cups medium rye flour
2 tablespoons grated orange peel
3½ to 4 cups all-purpose flour

Combine brown sugar, molasses, salt and shortening in small bowl; pour in boiling water. Stir mixture until sugar is dissolved. Cool to lukewarm (105°F. to 115°F.). Sprinkle yeast in warm water; stir to dissolve. Stir rye flour into brown sugar mixture. Add orange peel; beat until smooth. Stir in enough all-purpose flour to make smooth, soft dough. Turn dough onto floured surface; knead until smooth and elastic, about 10 minutes. Place dough in lightly greased large bowl; turn to grease top. Cover; let rise in warm place 1½ to 2 hours. Punch down dough; turn onto lightly floured surface. Divided in half; let rest 10 minutes. Grease 2 (8 x 4-inch) loaf pans. Shape dough into 2 loaves. Place in prepared pans. Cover and let rise until almost double, 1½ to 2 hours. Heat oven to 350°F. Bake 25 to 30 minutes or until loaves sound hollow when tapped. Remove from pans. Brush with butter for soft crust. Cool on rack.

New England Date Bread with Orange Cheese Log

1 (8 x 4-inch) Loaf

A family recipe from Fanny Farmer's Cooking School when Fanny herself was the teacher!

BREAD

1   (8-oz.) pkg. chopped dates
1   teaspoon baking soda
1   cup boiling water
1   tablespoon butter or margarine
¾ cup sugar
1   egg, beaten
1½ cups all-purpose flour
½ teaspoon salt

CHEESE LOG

1   (8-oz.) pkg. cream cheese, softened
1   teaspoon orange extract
    Grated peel of 1 orange
    Few drops orange liqueur, if desired
½ cup chopped walnuts

BREAD: Heat oven to 350°F. Grease 8 x 4-inch loaf pan. Combine dates, soda and water in large bowl; cool slightly. Stir in butter, sugar and egg. Combine flour and salt; blend into date mixture. Immediately pour into pan. (Dates will lose character if left in mixture too long.) Bake at 350°F. for 55 to 60 minutes or until toothpick inserted in center comes out clean. Cool 10 minutes in pan. Remove from pan; cool completely on rack. Serve with cream cheese log.

CHEESE LOG: Combine cream cheese, orange extract, peel and liqueur. Shape into log; roll in walnuts. Refrigerate to chill.

Rafferty's Golden Cheese Popovers

4 Popovers

A savory variation of traditional popovers.

⅔ cup all-purpose flour
¼ teaspoon salt
⅓ cup milk
⅓ cup water
2   eggs
1   oz. (¼ cup) shredded Cheddar cheese
1   to 1½ tablespoons shortening

Heat oven to 375°F. Combine flour and salt in medium bowl. Gradually add milk and water, blending well. Beat in eggs until smooth. Fold in cheese. Place about 1 teaspoon shortening in bottom of each of 4 (6-oz.) custard cups. Place cups on cookie sheet; heat in oven 3 to 5 minutes until shortening is melted and cups are hot. Fill cups ½ to ⅔ full. Bake at 375°F. for 45 to 50 minutes or until puffed and golden. Do not open oven while popovers are baking. Remove from custard cups; serve immediately.

Sour Cream Breakfast Bread

1 (9 x 5-inch) Loaf

TOPPING

½	cup sugar
½	cup chopped pecans
1	teaspoon cinnamon

BREAD

2	cups all-purpose flour
1	teaspoon baking powder
½	teaspoon baking soda
¼	teaspoon salt
1	cup butter or margarine, softened
1½	cups sugar
2	eggs
1	cup dairy sour cream
1	teaspoon vanilla

Heat oven to 350°F. Grease 9 x 5-inch loaf pan.
  TOPPING: Combine all topping ingredients; mix well.
  BREAD: Combine flour, baking powder, soda and salt in medium bowl.
Cream butter and 1½ cups sugar until light and fluffy. Add eggs one at a
time, beating well after each addition. Fold in sour cream and vanilla. Stir in
flour. Spoon ½ of batter into prepared pan. Sprinkle with ½ of topping.
Repeat layers. Tap pan on counter before baking. Bake at 350°F. for about
60 minutes or until toothpick inserted in center comes out clean. (If bread
begins to brown too much, cover lightly with foil.) Cool 10 minutes in pan.
Turn out onto rack to cool completely.

TIP: *Bread is best if made 1 day ahead of serving.*

Cheesy Onion Bread

6 to 10 Servings

Serve with a hearty soup or stew or a main dish salad.

8	oz. (2 cups) shredded Cheddar cheese
1	cup mayonnaise
1	bunch green onions, chopped
1	loaf French bread
	Grated Parmesan cheese
	Dried oregano leaves, crushed

Heat oven to 350°F. Cut French bread in half lengthwise. Combine shredded cheese, mayonnaise and onions; spread on cut side of bread. Sprinkle
with Parmesan cheese and oregano; place on cookie sheet. Bake at 350°F.
for 15 minutes. Slice and serve.

Pocket Cheese Bread

8 Servings

FILLING

1 egg, lightly beaten
1 lb. (4 cups) shredded Gruyere or Muenster cheese
2 tablespoons snipped fresh parsley, if desired
⅓ cup snipped fresh chives, if desired

BREAD

1 pkg. active dry yeast
2 teaspoons sugar
½ cup warm water (105 °F. to 115 °F.)
1 teaspoon salt
¼ cup butter or margarine, softened
1½ to 1¾ cups all-purpose flour

GLAZE

1 egg yolk
1 tablespoon water

FILLING: Combine all filling ingredients in medium bowl; mix well.

BREAD: Dissolve yeast and sugar in warm water. Allow mixture to become foamy. Combine yeast mixture, salt and butter in large bowl. Stir in enough flour to make a firm moist dough. Knead 3 to 4 minutes on lightly floured surface. Place dough in oiled bowl; turn to oil top. Cover and let rise in warm place 2 to 3 hours, until double. Punch down dough; roll out on lightly floured surface to 16-inch circle. Place in 8 or 9-inch pie plate. Fill with cheese mixture. Pull up excess dough. Pinch edges to form top crust.

GLAZE: Combine egg yolk and water; brush over crust. Allow to rest 15 to 20 minutes. Heat oven to 375 °F. Bake 15 to 20 minutes or until lightly brown. Cool. Serve warm or at room temperature.

Gustino's Pepperoni Bread

2 (9 x 5-inch) Loaves

Gustino's, Minneapolis,
Morano Dare

Gustino's, Minneapolis Mar-
riott, is a fun restaurant,
famous for its Italian food and
singing waiters.

6 to 7 cups all-purpose flour
½ oz. malt, if desired
   Dash salt
2 eggs
2 oz. compressed yeast
1 tablespoon butter or margarine, melted
2 cups milk
2 sticks pepperoni, skinned (same length as bread pan)
1 cup rolled oats
1 egg, beaten

Place flour in large bowl; make a well in center. Add malt, salt, eggs, yeast, butter and 1 cup milk. Gently incorporate into flour until dough becomes dry by kneading. Add a little more milk and resume kneading. Incorporate enough liquid so dough is easy to knead. (May be kneaded with dough hook on electric mixer.) Kneading must be done to ensure good light texture to bread; 10 minutes is necessary. Place mixture in buttered bowl; turn to grease top. Cover with damp towel; let rise in warm place until double. Grease 2 (9 x 5-inch) loaf pans. Punch dough down; knead 10 minutes. Cut dough in half; shape each piece into a loaf. Cut a slit down the length; insert a pepperoni stick. Brush with egg and sprinkle with oats. Place loaves in prepared pans. Let rise until double. Heat oven to 400 °F. Bake 15 to 20 minutes. Remove from pans. Cool on racks.

BREADS

Parmesan Cheese Bread

2 (9 x 5-inch) Loaves

For a savory spread, combine Parmesan cheese with softened butter.

2   pkg. active dry yeast
½   cup warm water (105 °F. to 115 °F.)
1   egg, beaten
¼   cup sugar
2   teaspoons salt
¼   cup butter or margarine, softened
1   cup lukewarm water
1   cup grated Parmesan cheese
6½ to 7 cups all-purpose flour
1   egg, well beaten
2   tablespoons sesame seeds

Dissolve yeast in ½ cup warm water. Combine 1 egg, sugar, salt, butter and 1 cup water with yeast. Stir in cheese and enough flour to make a stiff dough. Turn dough onto heavily floured surface; knead 10 minutes or until smooth and elastic. Place dough in greased bowl; turn to grease top. Let rise in warm place until double. Grease 2 (9 x 5-inch) loaf pans. Punch down dough and knead. Cut dough into 2 pieces; shape each into a 9-inch square. To shape loaves, roll each piece tightly, jelly-roll style. Place seam side down in prepared pans. Brush tops of loaves with egg; sprinkle with sesame seeds. Let rise until double. Heat oven to 375 °F. Bake 30 to 35 minutes or until loaves sound hollow when tapped. Remove from pans. Cool on rack. Slice when cooled to room temperature.

Pronto Ristorante's Rosemary Rolls

1 to 1½ Dozen

Pronto Ristorante, Minneapolis

If a softer crust is desired, brush rolls that are still warm with a little melted butter.

1   envelope active dry yeast
2   teaspoons sugar
1   cup warm water (105 °F. to 115 °F.)
2¾ cups all-purpose flour
1   teaspoon salt
2   teaspoons dried rosemary (or 1 tablespoon fresh rosemary)
⅓   cup olive oil
1   tablespoon coarse sea salt, optional

Dissolve yeast, sugar and ¼ cup warm water in a small bowl. Let stand 5 to 10 minutes until bubbly. If yeast does not bubble, discard and begin again. Place flour, salt and rosemary in food processor with steel blade. Process to mix. Add yeast mixture to flour and process 10 seconds or until blended. With processor running, slowly drizzle enough of the remaining water through feed tube into flour mixture so dough forms a ball that cleans the sides of the bowl. Process about 35 seconds. Let stand 1 minute. Turn on processor and gradually add a few more drops water to make dough soft and smooth, but not sticky. Process about 20 seconds. Turn dough onto lightly greased surface and form into ball. Place dough in lightly greased bowl, cover, and let rise in warm place 2 hours. Grease a cookie sheet and sprinkle generously with sea salt if desired. Punch dough down. Divide into 12 to 18 pieces; shape into round balls. Dip each ball into olive oil. Place on cookie sheet. Let rise until doubled. Heat oven to 350ºF. Bake about 25 minutes or until golden brown.

Blueberry Orange Bread

1 (9 x 5-inch) Loaf

*Delicious with fresh blue-
berries. Serve for a summer
brunch.*

1   cup sugar
½   teaspoon salt
1   cup water
    Grated peel of 1 large orange
2½ cups all-purpose flour
1   tablespoon baking powder
2   eggs
2   teaspoons vegetable oil
1   cup blueberries

Heat oven to 350°F. Grease and flour 9 x 5-inch loaf pan. Combine sugar, salt, water and orange peel in saucepan. Bring liquid to a boil. Measure syrup and add enough water to make 1½ cups; cool. Combine flour and baking powder in large bowl. Beat eggs and oil in separate bowl. Stir eggs, oil and sugar syrup into flour just until moistened. Fold in blueberries. Pour into prepared pan. Bake at 350°F. for about 1 hour or until well browned and toothpick inserted in center comes out clean. Cool 10 minutes in pan. Remove from pan; cool completely on rack.

Honey Lemon Whole Wheat Rolls

16 Rolls

*An easy yeast roll that can be
made ahead.*

1¾ to 2¼ cups all-purpose flour
1   pkg. active dry yeast
1½ teaspoons salt
1½ teaspoons grated lemon peel
2   tablespoons honey
1½ tablespoons butter or margarine, softened
1   cup plus 2 tablespoons hot tap water (105°F. to 115°F.)
1   cup stone ground whole wheat flour
    Cornmeal
    Vegetable oil

Combine 1 cup all-purpose flour, undissolved yeast, salt and lemon peel in large bowl; mix well. Add honey, butter and hot water. Beat 2 minutes on medium speed. Add ½ cup whole wheat flour and beat on high speed 1 minute or until thick and elastic. Stir in remaining whole wheat flour and enough all-purpose flour to form a soft dough. Knead until smooth and elastic, 5 to 10 minutes. Place in bowl; cover with plastic wrap and towel. Let rest 20 minutes. Grease 9-inch round pan; sprinkle with cornmeal. Punch dough down. Cut into 16 pieces; shape into balls. Place in prepared pan. Brush tops of rolls with oil. Cover with plastic wrap. Refrigerate 2 to 24 hours. Remove dough from refrigerator and let stand at room temperature 10 minutes. Heat oven to 400°F. Bake 25 to 30 minutes. Remove from pan. Cool on rack.

Cheese and Eggs

Warm Shrimp Flan with Riesling Sauce

6 Servings

Atrium Cafe International and Primavera, Minneapolis, Richard and Larry D'Amico

Atrium Cafe International is located in the atrium at International Market Square. A beautiful place for lunch.

Worth the effort when you need an elegant first course.

RIESLING SAUCE

2 cups Riesling wine
2 cups fish stock
2 shallots, minced
4 cups whipping cream
1 tablespoon lemon juice
  Salt and white pepper to taste
¼ cup cold unsalted butter

FLAN

1 lb. shrimp, peeled and deveined
1 egg white
  Juice of ½ lemon
⅓ to ½ cup whipping cream
  Salt and pepper
1 tablespoon minced carrot
1 tablespoon minced leek

SAUCE: Combine wine, stock and shallots in 2-quart saucepan; heat to boiling. Reduce heat and simmer to reduce liquid to 3 oz. (about ⅓ cup). Add 4 cups cream; simmer over medium heat until liquid is reduced by ¼ or until mixture coats back of spoon. Remove from heat. Season with 1 tablespoon lemon juice, salt and pepper. Cut cold butter into walnut-size pieces; stir into sauce until melted. Keep covered until serving time.

FLAN: Grease 6 ramekins or small molds. Combine shrimp, egg white and lemon juice in food processor; puree. Refrigerate mixture to chill. Slowly add ⅓ to ½ cup cream to shrimp mixture and mix well. Salt and pepper to taste. Fold vegetables into shrimp mixture; pour into prepared ramekins. Cover and place ramekins on rack in pan containing 1 to 2 inches boiling water; steam 10 to 12 minutes or until toothpick inserted in center comes out clean. Remove ramekins to warm serving plate. Serve with Riesling sauce.

Black-Eyed Susan Eggs

4 Servings

1 medium onion, chopped
2 tablespoons butter or margarine
4 eggs, beaten
6 large pitted ripe olives, coarsely chopped
2 oz. Provolone cheese, finely diced
2 tablespoons grated Parmesan cheese
  Salt and pepper

Saute onion in butter in large skillet until tender. Combine eggs, olives, cheeses, salt and pepper in medium bowl. Pour into skillet with onion; cook, stirring over low heat until eggs are lightly scrambled and cheeses melt. Serve immediately.

Oeufs Pouches Maintenon

4 Servings

Hotel Sofitel, Bloomington, Daniel Hubert

Hotel Sofitel features three French restaurants: Chéz Colette, Le Café Royal and La Terrasse.

MUSHROOM PUREE

1   shallot, finely chopped
2   tablespoons butter or margarine
2   lb. fresh mushrooms, finely chopped
    Salt and pepper to taste
    Juice of ½ lemon
1   cup whipping cream

HOLLANDAISE SAUCE

¾   cup plus 2 tablespoons butter
    Juice of ½ lemon
    Water
3   egg yolks
    Salt and pepper
    Dash cayenne pepper

EGGS

8   eggs
    Vinegar
    Heart-shaped croutons, if desired

PUREE: Saute shallot in 2 tablespoons butter for 1 to 2 minutes. Add mushrooms, salt, pepper and juice of ½ lemon; cook until liquid from mushrooms has evaporated. Stir in cream; cook until liquid is reduced by half.

HOLLANDAISE SAUCE: Melt butter; pour off clear liquid. Discard milky solids. Combine ¾ of lemon juice and an equal amount of water in small bowl with egg yolks; whip well. Salt and pepper to taste. Place mixture in top of double boiler over hot water. Whip constantly until mixture is frothy; remove from heat. Whip in clarified butter a little at a time. Whip in remaining lemon juice and cayenne.

EGGS: Poach eggs in water with a small amount of vinegar. Divide mushroom puree on 4 plates. Place 2 eggs on top of puree and cover with hollandaise sauce. Garnish with heart-shaped croutons.

Dutch Baby Souffle

2 Servings

Perfect for breakfast. Great with sauteed apple slices.

¼ cup butter or margarine
3 eggs
¾ cup milk
¾ cup all-purpose flour
   Powdered sugar
   Lemon slices

Heat oven to 425 °F. Place butter in 2 to 3-quart casserole or souffle dish. Place casserole in oven to melt butter. Place eggs in blender or food processor; blend at high speed 1 minute. While blender is running, pour in milk and flour. Blend 30 seconds longer. Pour batter into hot casserole. Bake at 425 °F. for 20 to 25 minutes or until puffed. Sprinkle with powdered sugar and garnish with lemon slices.

Wild Rice Quiche

6 to 8 Servings

⅓ cup julienne strips of Canadian bacon
1 small onion, diced
1 (9-inch) unbaked pie shell
4 oz. (1 cup) shredded Monterey Jack cheese
1 cup cooked wild rice
3 eggs
1½ cups half-and-half
½ teaspoon salt
   Dash hot pepper sauce

Heat oven to 350 °F. Fry Canadian bacon and onion until onion is translucent; drain. Spread mixture evenly in pie shell. Sprinkle with cheese and wild rice. Whip eggs, half-and-half, salt and hot pepper sauce; pour over wild rice. Bake at 350 °F. for 50 minutes or until center is set.

Frittata Rosolini

4 Servings

6 slices bacon, chopped
½ cup diced onion
1 cup thinly sliced zucchini
1 (10-oz.) pkg. frozen chopped spinach, cooked and well drained
½ teaspoon dried oregano leaves, crumbled
   Salt and pepper
6 eggs
¾ cup whipping cream
   Prepared mild salsa

Fry bacon; drain, reserving ¼ cup drippings. Heat oven to 350 °F. Saute onion and zucchini in ovenproof skillet in reserved drippings. Combine bacon, onion, zucchini, spinach, oregano, salt and pepper to taste in skillet. Whip eggs with cream and pour over vegetables. Bake at 350 °F. for 30 minutes. Serve with salsa.

Brunch Casserole Olé

6 Servings

1 (4-oz.) can chopped green chilies, drained
8 oz. (2 cups) shredded Cheddar cheese
2 eggs
1 (12-oz.) can evaporated milk
2 tablespoons cornmeal
  Dash salt
1½ teaspoons Worcestershire sauce
8 oz. (2 cups) shredded Monterey Jack cheese
1 (8-oz.) can tomato sauce

Heat oven to 350°F. Arrange ½ of chilies in bottom of 8 or 9-inch square pan. Sprinkle ½ of Cheddar cheese over chilies. Sprinkle remaining chilies over cheese and cover with remaining Cheddar cheese. Combine eggs, milk, cornmeal, salt and Worcestershire sauce; beat well. Pour mixture over chilies and cheese. Bake at 350°F. for 30 minutes. Add ½ of the Monterey Jack cheese, tomato sauce and top with remaining cheese. Continue to bake for 15 minutes longer. Let stand 10 to 15 minutes before serving. Cut into squares.

Eggs Florentine

12 Servings

4 oz. (1 cup) shredded Cheddar cheese
1 (10-oz.) pkg. frozen chopped spinach, cooked and well drained
1 (12-oz.) roll well-seasoned pork sausage
6 oz. fresh mushrooms, sliced
½ cup chopped scallions
2 tablespoons butter or margarine
12 eggs, slightly beaten
2 cups whipping cream
4 oz. (1 cup) shredded Swiss cheese
  Paprika

TIP: *Casserole can be prepared, covered and refrigerated or frozen. Bring to room temperature to bake. If frozen, remove from freezer the night before. Bake as directed in recipe.*

Heat oven to 350°F. Grease 13 x 9-inch pan. Spread Cheddar cheese in prepared pan. Spread spinach evenly over cheese. Fry sausage until no longer pink; drain and crumble over spinach. Saute mushrooms and scallions in butter; sprinkle over sausage. Beat eggs with cream; pour into pan. Top with Swiss cheese; sprinkle with paprika. Bake at 350°F. for 30 to 40 minutes or until set.

Eggs Prescott

8 Servings

8 eggs, beaten
1 cup milk
1 teaspoon sugar
½ teaspoon salt
8 oz. (2 cups) shredded Monterey Jack cheese
1 (3-oz.) pkg. cream cheese, cut into small cubes
1 cup cottage cheese
3 tablespoons butter or margarine, softened
½ cup all-purpose flour
1 teaspoon baking powder

TIP: *Egg-cheese mixture can be prepared 1 day before serving; cover and refrigerate. Add flour and baking powder just before baking.*

Heat oven to 325°F. Butter 13 x 9-inch pan. Combine eggs, milk, sugar and salt in bowl; blend in cheeses and butter. Combine flour and baking powder; stir into egg mixture. Pour into prepared pan. Bake at 325°F. for 40 minutes or until set. Let stand 5 to 7 minutes before serving.

Baked Eggs with Muenster Cheese

8 Servings

St. Paul Hotel, St. Paul, John Geschrei

Serve with smoked or cured salmon.

2 tablespoons butter or margarine, softened
4 medium tomatoes, sliced ¼-inch thick
8 (⅛-inch) thick slices Muenster cheese
8 eggs
4 cups whipping cream
2 tablespoons snipped fresh basil leaves
  Salt and freshly ground pepper

Heat oven to 350°F. Butter 13 x 9-inch casserole. Completely cover bottom of casserole with tomato slices. Cover tomatoes with cheese slices, overlapping if necessary. Break eggs individually over cheese slices, spacing them evenly in casserole. Scald cream; pour carefully over eggs. Sprinkle with basil; salt and pepper to taste. Bake at 350°F. for 30 minutes or until eggs appear soft-set. Serve immediately.

Entrées

Breast of Chicken with Fontina
(Petti di Pollo alla Modena)

4 Servings

2 whole chicken breasts, skinned, halved and boned
   Salt and pepper
½ cup all-purpose flour
¼ cup butter or margarine
¼ cup olive oil
12 thin slices prosciutto ham
12 slices Fontina cheese
½ cup grated Parmesan cheese

Heat oven to 350 °F. Slice each chicken breast half into 3 equal slices; salt and pepper to taste. Dip chicken into flour; shake off excess. Saute chicken in butter and oil, 1 to 2 minutes per side. Transfer to shallow baking pan. (Chicken can be prepared ahead to this point and refrigerated.) Place 1 slice prosciutto and 1 slice cheese on each serving. Sprinkle lightly with Parmesan cheese. Bake, uncovered, at 350 °F. for 10 to 20 minutes. Serve with Italian broad beans, sauteed in lemon juice with minced garlic, if desired.

Chinese Chili Pepper Chicken

4 Servings

½ teaspoon salt
¼ teaspoon pepper
1 teaspoon cornstarch
1 egg white, beaten
4 whole chicken breasts, skinned, boned and cut into large pieces
⅓ cup peanut oil
½ teaspoon ground ginger
¼ teaspoon crushed red pepper
2 teaspoons sugar
½ teaspoon salt
2½ tablespoons cider vinegar
2 tablespoons dark soy sauce
1 tablespoon dry sherry
   Cooked white rice, if desired

Combine ½ teaspoon salt, pepper, cornstarch and egg white. Coat chicken with mixture and let stand 30 minutes. Heat oil in wok over high heat. Add chicken and stir-fry about 2½ minutes; remove chicken and drain. Reserve 2 tablespoons oil in wok; add ginger, red pepper and chicken. Stir briskly until chicken is thoroughly cooked. Add remaining ingredients except rice to wok. Stir until chicken is coated. Serve over white rice.

Chicken Neapolitan

6 Servings

1 egg
½ cup milk
2 tablespoons olive oil
1 cup Italian seasoned bread crumbs
3 whole chicken breasts, skinned, halved, boned and pounded flat
6 large fresh mushrooms, cut into thick slices
6 (¼-inch) slices Mozzarella cheese
1 (15-oz.) can tomato sauce
½ teaspoon dried basil leaves, crushed
½ teaspoon ground oregano
¼ teaspoon garlic powder
⅓ cup grated Parmesan cheese

Heat oven to 375°F. Beat egg and milk together in medium bowl. Heat oil in skillet over medium heat. Place bread crumbs in separate bowl. Dip chicken breasts, one at a time, into egg mixture, then crumbs. Shake off excess crumbs. Saute chicken in skillet until brown. Transfer chicken to 13 x 9-inch baking dish; top with mushrooms and Mozzarella cheese. Combine tomato sauce and seasonings; pour over chicken. Sprinkle with Parmesan cheese. (Chicken can be prepared ahead to this point and refrigerated.) Bake at 375°F. for 20 to 30 minutes. Serve with pasta or noodles and a green salad, if desired.

Chicken Broccoli Casserole

6 to 8 Servings

2 (8-oz.) pkg. cream cheese
2 cups milk
1 teaspoon salt
½ teaspoon garlic salt
½ cup grated Parmesan cheese
2 (10-oz.) pkg. frozen broccoli spears, thawed and well drained
4 whole chicken breasts, cooked, skinned and boned
Paprika
½ cup grated Parmesan cheese

Heat oven to 350°F. Grease 13 x 9-inch baking dish. Combine cream cheese, milk, salt, garlic salt and ½ cup Parmesan cheese in blender; mix well. Transfer mixture to saucepan and cook over medium heat, stirring constantly until thick. Layer broccoli, half of sauce, chicken and remaining sauce in prepared baking dish. Sprinkle with remaining Parmesan cheese and paprika. Bake at 350°F. for 25 to 30 minutes.

Patio Chicken

6 to 12 Servings

Delicious hot or cold. Pack for a gourmet picnic!

- 1 cup dry bread crumbs
- 1½ teaspoons onion salt
- ½ teaspoon pepper
- ½ teaspoon garlic powder
- ½ teaspoon summer savory
- ½ teaspoon curry powder
- 1 to 2 (2½ to 3-lb.) frying chickens, cut up (skinned, if desired)
- ½ to 1 cup mayonnaise

Heat oven to 400°F. Combine crumbs and seasonings in plastic bag. Add chicken pieces, one at a time, and shake to coat. Place chicken in shallow baking pan. Bake at 400°F. for 15 minutes. Brush with mayonnaise. Reduce oven temperature to 325°F. Bake 1 hour longer, or until tender. Serve hot or cold.

Chicken Marengo with Gnocchi

6 Servings

- 2½ to 3-lb. frying chicken
- 1 teaspoon salt
- 1 teaspoon pepper
- ¼ cup butter
- 3 small onions, chopped
- 1 clove garlic, minced
- ½ cup chicken broth
- ½ cup dry white wine
- 1½ cups canned Italian tomatoes, drained and quartered
- 2 sprigs fresh parsley
- 1 celery stalk, coarsely chopped
- 1 bay leaf
- ½ teaspoon dried thyme leaves, crushed
- 3 medium onions, cut into quarters
- 8 oz. whole fresh mushrooms, sauteed
- 3 tablespoons cornstarch
- ⅓ cup water
- Snipped fresh parsley

GNOCCHI

- 1 cup water
- ½ cup butter or margarine
- 1 teaspoon salt
- 1 cup all-purpose flour
- 4 eggs
- 1 oz. (¼ cup) shredded Swiss cheese
- 1 teaspoon dry mustard
- Dash nutmeg
- Dash cayenne pepper
- 2 tablespoons butter or margarine, melted
- ½ cup grated Parmesan cheese

(Continued)

(Chicken Marengo with Gnocchi *continued*)

Cut chicken into serving pieces. Remove skin and pat chicken dry. Sprinkle with 1 teaspoon salt and pepper. Melt ¼ cup butter in heavy Dutch oven. Add chicken and brown over medium heat. Remove chicken. Add chopped onions; saute until lightly brown. Add garlic, chicken broth and white wine. Heat to boiling, scraping particles from bottom of pan. Add tomatoes, parsley, celery, bay leaf and thyme. Return chicken to pan; simmer about 30 minutes. Add quartered onions and sauteed mushrooms. Remove parsley and bay leaf. Combine cornstarch and ⅓ cup water. Remove chicken and vegetables to platter. Thicken sauce with a portion of cornstarch mixture; season to taste. Pour sauce over chicken. Sprinkle with snipped parsley. Serve with gnocchi.

GNOCCHI: Heat oven to 350 °F. Grease 13 x 9-inch baking dish. Combine 1 cup water, ½ cup butter and 1 teaspoon salt in saucepan; heat to boiling. Remove from heat; stir in flour. Return to heat and beat with wooden spoon until mixture forms a small ball, about 1 minute. Remove from heat. Add eggs one at a time, beating well after each addition. Stir in Swiss cheese, mustard, nutmeg and cayenne. Drop gnocchi, 1 tablespoon at a time, into pan of simmering water; cook about ⅓ of dough at a time. Simmer 8 to 9 minutes. Remove with skimmer; drain. Arrange single layer of gnocchi in prepared baking dish. Drizzle with melted butter; sprinkle with Parmesan cheese. Bake at 350 °F. for about 20 minutes. (Use broiler for final browning if necessary.)

TIP: To simplify preparation, buy fresh gnocchi from a specialty store or serve with buttered pasta or mashed potatoes.

Pollo di Selvaggio

4 Servings

Pronto Ristorante, Hyatt Hotel, Minneapolis

4	boneless chicken breast halves, pounded thin
	Flour
2	to 4 tablespoons butter or margarine
1½	cups whipping cream
3	oz. goat cheese, preferably Bucheron
4	oz. sun-dried tomatoes, soaked and julienned
4	oz. wild mushrooms, porcini or oyster
	Salt and pepper

Lightly flour chicken. Saute in butter until lightly browned. Drain off excess butter. Stir in cream, cheese, tomatoes and mushrooms. Break up cheese to blend well with cream; reduce mixture. Cook over medium heat 10 to 20 minutes or until chicken is tender. Remove chicken and keep warm. Continue to cook cream until reduced to sauce consistency. Salt and pepper to taste; pour over chicken.

TIP: Use fresh wild mushrooms if you can find them. Dried mushrooms must be rinsed thoroughly and soaked up to 2 hours. Their special flavor is worth the extra expense.

Glazed Game Hens

4 Servings

Two great glazes for roast game hens.

Mustard Curry or Orange Currant Glaze (recipes follow)
4   Cornish game hens
Salt and pepper

Heat oven to 375 °F. Prepare one of the glazes. Clean game hens. Sprinkle insides with salt and pepper (stuff if desired); place in shallow roasting pan. Roast at 375 °F. for 1 hour, basting with glaze every 15 minutes.

Orange Currant Glaze

*2 Cups Glaze
(enough for 4 to 6 game hens)*

2   oranges, peeled and quartered
½   cup butter or margarine, melted
1   (10-oz.) jar currant jelly
1   (6-oz.) can frozen orange juice concentrate, thawed
Garlic salt
Salt and pepper to taste

Place oranges in cavities of game hens. Combine remaining ingredients in medium bowl. Baste hens while roasting.

Mustard Curry Glaze

*1⅓ Cups Glaze
(enough for 4 to 6 game hens)*

⅔   cup dark corn syrup
½   cup prepared mustard
3   teaspoons curry powder
1   teaspoon salt
2   cloves garlic, minced

Combine all ingredients in small bowl. Baste game hens while roasting.

Chicken Enchiladas

4 to 5 Servings

This entree is very spicy!

2   whole chicken breasts, skinned
1   small onion

SAUCE

6   green bell peppers, skinned and seeded
1   (4-oz.) can hot Mexican chilies
1½ cups whipping cream
1   egg
2   (4-oz.) cans mild green chilies
5   teaspoons snipped fresh coriander or parsley
    Salt and pepper to taste

6   oz. cream cheese, softened
½   cup whipping cream
¾   cup finely chopped onion
8   to 10 flour tortillas
8   oz. (2 cups) shredded Monterey Jack cheese

HINT: *To easily remove pepper skins, refer to recipe on page 69 for instructions.*

TIP: *Enchiladas can be rolled ahead of time. Do not add sauce until ready to bake.*

Poach chicken in water to cover, with small onion, 20 to 30 minutes or until tender. Reserve ¼ cup chicken stock. Cool chicken slightly; cut into cubes.

SAUCE: Combine all sauce ingredients with ¼ cup reserved chicken stock in blender or food processor; blend 10 seconds.

Heat oven to 350 °F. Grease large baking dish. Combine cream cheese, whipping cream, chopped onion and chicken; set aside. Dip tortillas in sauce; fry lightly in hot oil in skillet. Fill with chicken mixture; roll up and place in prepared baking dish. Pour remaining sauce over tortillas; sprinkle with shredded cheese. Bake at 350 °F. for 35 to 40 minutes.

Orange Baked Pheasant

4 Servings

Michael J. Douglas, "Donuts" of KS95-FM, submitted this recipe which he also uses for chicken.

2½ to 3-lb. pheasant, cleaned and cut up
    Flour
    Butter or margarine
1   (6-oz.) can frozen orange juice concentrate, thawed
¼   cup packed brown sugar
¼   teaspoon ground ginger
    Salt and pepper

Heat oven to 375 °F. Coat pheasant pieces with flour. Melt butter in skillet; brown pheasant. Place pheasant pieces in baking dish. Combine orange juice concentrate, brown sugar and ginger; pour over pheasant. Salt and pepper to taste. Bake at 375 °F. for 45 to 50 minutes.

Cajun Seafood Stew

8 Servings

Serve with crusty French bread for dunking!

2 tablespoons olive oil
2 green peppers, cut into bite-size pieces
1 bunch green onions, including tops, chopped
3 to 4 cloves garlic, minced
1 lb. fresh mushrooms, sliced
2 (6-oz.) cans minced clams, undrained
2 (16-oz.) cans stewed tomatoes
1 (8-oz.) can tomato sauce with herbs
¼ teaspoon dried oregano leaves, crushed
¼ teaspoon dried basil leaves, crushed
1 tablespoon Cajun Magic seasoning
   Black pepper to taste
1 lb. baby bay scallops
1 lb. white fish fillets
½ lb. medium shrimp, peeled and deveined
½ cup white wine, if desired

Heat oil in large saucepan. Add green peppers, green onions, garlic and mushrooms; saute about 5 minutes. Stir in clams, tomatoes, tomato sauce, oregano, basil, Cajun Magic and black pepper. Heat to boiling; reduce heat and simmer 15 minutes. Stir in scallops, fish, shrimp and white wine. Cook 15 to 20 minutes longer.

Gulf Shrimp in Wine

4 Servings

St. James Hotel, Red Wing, Charles Worth

1 lb. fresh jumbo shrimp, peeled and deveined
2 tablespoons unsalted butter
¼ teaspoon salt
⅛ teaspoon white pepper
¼ teaspoon snipped fresh basil leaves
¼ teaspoon snipped fresh oregano leaves
½ teaspoon minced shallot
½ teaspoon minced garlic
¼ cup julienne onion strips
4 fresh medium mushrooms, sliced
2 small tomatoes, peeled and quartered
8 ripe olives
2 tablespoons dry white wine
   Juice of ½ lemon
1½ cups whipping cream
2 tablespoons unsalted butter

Saute shrimp in 2 tablespoons butter; stir in salt, pepper, fresh herbs, vegetables and olives. Deglaze pan with white wine. Stir in lemon juice, cream and remaining butter; reduce heat and simmer until well blended and thoroughly heated. Serve with wild and white rice mixture, if desired.

Whole Grilled Salmon with Dill Sauce

8 to 12 Servings

An impressive presentation for a special dinner.

DILL SAUCE

- 1½ cups dairy sour cream
- ½ cup mayonnaise
- 1½ tablespoons snipped fresh dill (or 1 tablespoon dried dill weed)
- 1 teaspoon grated onion
- ½ teaspoon salt
- ¼ teaspoon pepper

SALMON

- 6 to 8-lb. fresh whole salmon
  Salt and pepper to taste
- 2 tablespoons butter or margarine, softened
- ½ medium onion, sliced
- 1 lemon, sliced
- 2 tablespoons vegetable oil

  Lemon slices or wedges
  Fresh parsley sprigs
  Fresh dill sprigs

SAUCE: Combine all sauce ingredients; mix well. Cover; refrigerate overnight.

SALMON: Heat barbecue grill. Wash salmon and pat dry. Sprinkle inside with salt and pepper; dot with butter. Place onion and lemon inside fish cavity; brush outside with oil. Wrap fish in heavy-duty foil; seal. Grill over medium-hot coals, carefully turning every 10 minutes. Check after 30 to 35 minutes to see if fish flakes easily with fork at thickest part. Continue cooking until desired doneness is reached. Remove from grill. Working with the grain, skin and trim fish, removing fins and gray fatty portions until just pink flesh is left. Turn fish over; transfer to platter. Remove skin and fins from other side. Garnish platter with lemon, parsley and dill. Serve with dill sauce.

TIP: *For ease in serving, strip fish from bones with a large fork. When top layer is gone, remove all bones by grasping rib cage and gently lifting; second layer is ready to serve.*

Paupiettes de Sole with Blender Hollandaise

4 Servings

FISH

1   sheet frozen puff pastry, thawed
8   (3-oz.) sole fillets
    Pepper to taste
4   oz. smoked salmon, cut into small pieces
    Pepper to taste
2   tablespoons butter or margarine, softened
½   teaspoon lemon juice
1   egg yolk, slightly beaten

HOLLANDAISE

3   egg yolks, at room temperature
2   tablespoons lemon juice
2   tablespoons butter or margarine
¼   teaspoon salt
    Dash freshly ground black pepper
½   cup butter or margarine

FISH: Cut pastry into 4 squares. Roll each into an 8-inch square on lightly floured surface. Place 1 fillet on center of each square. Pepper lightly; set aside. Combine salmon, pepper, butter and lemon juice in blender or food processor until smooth. Spread mixture on fillets on pastry. Top with remaining fillets. Bring pastry up around fish to cover completely. Trim excess pastry with scissors. Pinch seams to seal. Place seam side down on non-stick cookie sheet. Refrigerate several hours or overnight. Heat oven to 400°F. Brush pastry with beaten egg yolk; bake at 400°F. in bottom ⅓ of oven for 20 to 25 minutes or until golden brown. Serve immediately with hollandaise sauce.

    HOLLANDAISE: Combine egg yolks, lemon juice, 2 tablespoons butter, salt and pepper in blender or food processor until well mixed. Melt ½ cup butter. With machine running, add hot butter in slow, steady stream. Mix just until smooth and thickened. Serve immediately or keep warm in thermos or in double broiler over steaming water.

Minnesota Walleye and Wild Rice

6 to 8 Servings

Byerly's, St. Louis Park

A Minnesota specialty from Byerly's Supermarket.

MUSHROOM-WALNUT SAUCE

3 tablespoons butter or margarine
1 tablespoon minced shallot
1 cup sliced fresh mushrooms
3 tablespoons flour
½ teaspoon dry mustard
½ teaspoon salt
¼ teaspoon dried thyme leaves, crumbled
2 cups half-and-half
¼ cup chopped walnuts, toasted

FILLETS

2 lb. walleye fillets
1 teaspoon salt
¼ teaspoon pepper
4 slices bacon, diced
1 cup chopped fresh mushrooms
¼ cup minced onion
⅓ cup minced celery
2½ cups cooked wild rice
2 tablespoons snipped fresh parsley
½ teaspoon salt
2 tablespoons butter or margarine, melted
3 tablespoons snipped fresh parsley

SAUCE: Melt 3 tablespoons butter in saucepan; saute shallot and sliced mushrooms until tender. Blend in flour, mustard, ½ teaspoon salt and thyme. Gradually stir in half-and-half. Cook over medium heat, stirring constantly, until mixture boils; boil and stir 1 minute. Stir in walnuts.

FILLETS: Heat oven to 350°F. Grease 13 x 9-inch pan. Cut fillets into serving size portions: place in prepared pan. Sprinkle fillets with 1 teaspoon salt and pepper. Fry bacon in medium-size skillet until lightly browned. Stir in chopped mushrooms, onion and celery; cook until tender. Stir in cooked wild rice, 2 tablespoons parsley and ½ teaspoon salt. Spoon heaping ½ cup of rice mixture on top of each fillet. Drizzle melted butter over rice. Bake, covered, at 350°F. for about 20 minutes or until fish flakes easily with fork. To serve, transfer to dinner plates with long pancake turner. Spoon a dollop of mushroom-walnut sauce over rice. Sprinkle with 3 tablespoons parsley. Pass remaining sauce.

Scallops with Sweet Red Pepper Cream

6 Servings

*The Studio Restaurant,
Minneapolis, Martha Geffen*

RED PEPPER PUREE

2	tablespoons butter
1	lb. sweet red peppers, diced
1	tablespoon sugar
1	tablespoon cider vinegar
1	teaspoon paprika
¼	teaspoon crushed hot red pepper
	Dash salt

SCALLOPS

2	tablespoons butter or margarine
1½	lb. bay scallops, rinsed
	Salt and pepper
½	cup white wine
2	tablespoons dry sherry
½	cup whipping cream
¼	cup snipped fresh parsley

RED PEPPER PUREE: Melt 2 tablespoons butter in saucepan over low heat. Add peppers, sugar, vinegar, paprika, hot red pepper and salt. Cover and cook until peppers are very soft, about 45 minutes. Uncover; increase heat and cook, stirring until liquid evaporates, about 10 minutes. Puree in blender or food processor.

SCALLOPS: Heat 2 tablespoons butter in saute pan until hot. Saute scallops just until they turn opaque. Transfer scallops to bowl. Salt and pepper to taste. Combine white wine and sherry in saucepan used for scallops. Cook until mixture is reduced to syrup. Whisk in cream and liquid accumulated from scallops. Boil mixture until thick or of sauce consistency. Combine sauce with pepper puree; mix well. Serve scallops on large platter. Mask with sauce. Garnish with snipped parsley.

TIP: *Puree can be made in advance.*

Vera Cruz Fish Fillets

4 Servings

Use fresh Minnesota walleye with this great topping.

VERA CRUZ TOPPING

1 avocado, peeled and finely diced
1 tomato, peeled, seeded and diced
¼ cup chopped scallions, including tops
½ teaspoon salt
   Pepper
5 to 6 dashes hot pepper sauce
2 tablespoons lemon juice
2 teaspoons vegetable oil

4 fresh fish fillets
   Salt and pepper
   Melted butter or margarine

TIP: *Topping can be prepared ahead except for avocado. Add avocado just before serving.*

TOPPING: Combine all topping ingredients in medium bowl; set aside.
    Heat broiler. Butter shallow baking dish; place fillets in dish. Salt and pepper to taste; brush with butter. Broil 10 minutes or until fish flakes easily with fork. Place fillets on serving plates; top with Vera Cruz topping. Serve with saffron rice, if desired.

Simply Superb Scallops

4 Servings

The title says it all.

1½ lb. sea scallops, cut in half horizontally
¼   cup butter or margarine, melted
3   tablespoons dry bread crumbs
⅛   teaspoon garlic salt
⅛   teaspoon dry mustard
½   teaspoon paprika
1   tablespoon butter or margarine, melted
2   tablespoons dry sherry
    Lemon slices

Heat broiler. Rinse scallops and pat dry. Pour ¼ cup butter into broiler platter or pan. Add scallops; turn to coat. Combine bread crumbs and seasonings; sprinkle over scallops. Drizzle with 1 tablespoon butter. Brown scallops under broiler 5 to 7 minutes. Turn off broiler and let scallops heat 3 minutes longer. Sprinkle with a few drops of sherry. Serve hot, garnished with lemon slices.

Salmon Mousse with Green Mayonnaise

4 to 6 Servings

MOUSSE

1 envelope unflavored gelatin
¼ cup cold water
½ cup boiling water
1 lb. cooked salmon or 1 (15-oz.) can salmon, drained and flaked
1 tablespoon prepared horseradish
1 tablespoon fresh lemon juice
Salt and freshly ground pepper to taste
3 to 4 drops hot pepper sauce
1 cup whipping cream, whipped

GREEN MAYONNAISE

1 cup mayonnaise
⅓ cup finely chopped watercress
2 tablespoons snipped fresh parsley
Fresh parsley sprigs
Cherry tomato halves
Green olive slices

MOUSSE: Sprinkle gelatin in cold water to soften. Stir in boiling water until gelatin is dissolved. Stir in salmon, horseradish, lemon juice, salt, pepper and hot pepper sauce. Refrigerate mixture until consistency of unbeaten egg whites. Fold in whipped cream. Pour into oiled fish mold. Refrigerate 4 to 6 hours or until firm.

MAYONNAISE: Combine all mayonnaise ingredients in small bowl; mix well. Refrigerate at least 1 hour. Unmold salmon mousse; garnish with parsley, cherry tomatoes, green olives and green mayonnaise.

Grilled Swordfish Steaks

4 to 6 Servings

Spice up your barbecue!

BASTING SAUCE

¼ cup butter or margarine
2 teaspoons Pickapeppa Sauce
½ teaspoon garlic salt
½ teaspoon instant minced onion
½ teaspoon Worcestershire sauce
¼ teaspoon hot pepper sauce

2 lb. fresh swordfish steaks

TIP: *Pickapeppa sauce is a spicy Cajun blend. It can be found in most gourmet specialty shops.*

Heat barbecue grill. Melt butter in small saucepan; stir in remaining sauce ingredients. Baste steaks with sauce. Grill 7 to 10 minutes per side or until fish flakes easily with fork. Baste occasionally while grilling.

Salmon Wellington

4 Servings

*The Fifth Season, Min-
neapolis, Anthony Harrington*

*The Fifth Season, in the City
Center Marriot, is a place for
special celebrations. Use this
recipe for one of your own.*

SPINACH FILLING

1   tablespoon butter or margarine
1   teaspoon chopped shallot
¼   cup white wine
    Dash nutmeg
8   oz. fresh spinach leaves, washed and stemmed

LOBSTER MOUSSE

8   oz. lobster or any white fish, chopped
2   egg whites
¼   cup whipping cream
2   tablespoons vermouth
1   tablespoon truffle peel or caviar
    Salt and pepper

4   (5 to 6½-inch) sheets frozen puff pastry, thawed
2   egg yolks, slightly beaten
8   (2½-oz.) fresh salmon fillets
¼   cup butter or margarine, melted
    Salt and pepper

FILLING: Melt 1 tablespoon butter in saucepan over low heat. Saute shallot until transparent; do not brown. Stir in wine and nutmeg. Add spinach leaves, turning frequently until incorporated into the mixture, 3 to 4 minutes. (Spinach should appear more wilted than cooked.) Cool.

MOUSSE: Combine lobster, egg whites, cream and vermouth in blender or food processor. Blend until mixture forms smooth paste. Blend in truffle peel. Salt and pepper to taste. Heat oven to 375 °F. Grease cookie sheet. Place pastry on lightly floured surface. Brush around edges of shells with egg yolk. Place 1 oz. spinach filling in center of each square. Place 1 salmon fillet on top of spinach mixture. Lightly brush with butter, sprinkle with salt and pepper. Add about ¼ of the lobster mousse; butter lightly. Salt and pepper. Place second salmon fillet over mousse; butter lightly. Salt and pepper. Fold 1 corner of pastry over salmon, bringing point to center. Bring remaining corners of pastry to center. Trim off any excess pastry. Brush pastry with egg yolk to seal. Garnish tops of filled pastry squares with cut-outs from excess pastry; brush with egg yolk. Bake at 375 °F. for 15 to 20 minutes.

Salmon Fillets with Lemon Dill Sauce

8 Servings

FISH STOCK

1 small carrot, diced
1 stalk celery, diced
3 green onions
¼ cup dry white wine
1¼ cups water
½ teaspoon salt
¼ teaspoon grated lemon peel
½ clove garlic
5 peppercorns
4 cups fish bones or pieces

LEMON DILL SAUCE

3 tablespoons butter or margarine
3 tablespoons flour
½ cup whipping cream
2 tablespoons lemon juice
½ teaspoon salt
½ teaspoon dried dill weed

8 fresh Norwegian salmon fillets
  Melted butter or margarine
  Lemon juice
  Salt and pepper
  Parsley flakes
  Dried dill weed
  Fennel
8 lemon wedges

STOCK: Combine all stock ingredients in large saucepan. Heat to boiling; reduce heat and simmer 20 minutes. Strain, reserving stock.

SAUCE: Melt 3 tablespoons butter in small saucepan; blend in flour. Gradually stir in 1¼ cups fish stock; cook until thickened. Remove from heat; stir in cream, lemon juice, salt and dill weed. Heat oven to 350 °F. Grease shallow baking dish; place fillets in dish. Brush with melted butter and lemon juice; sprinkle with salt, pepper, parsley flakes, dill weed and fennel. Bake at 350 °F. for 25 to 30 minutes or until salmon flakes easily with fork. Pour lemon dill sauce over fillets on dinner plate. Garnish with lemon wedges.

TIP: *One fish-flavor bouillon cube dissolved in 1¼ cups boiling water can be substituted for fish stock.*

Jumbo Prawns Voltaire

4 Servings

Cook at tableside to impress your friends. Serve with rice pilaf and fresh vegetables.

BECHAMEL SAUCE WITH CURRY

¼ cup butter or margarine
2 to 3 tablespoons curry powder
¼ cup flour
2 cups boiling milk
4 to 6 tablespoons whipping cream
   Salt and pepper
   Lemon juice

SHRIMP

½ cup chopped onion
4 oz. fresh mushrooms, sliced
½ cup butter or margarine
24 large prawns, peeled and deveined
   Dash salt and freshly ground pepper
   Dash sugar
   Dash garlic powder
¼ cup dairy sour cream
2 tablespoons brandy, warmed

SAUCE: Melt ¼ cup butter in saucepan over low heat. Stir in curry powder; cook slowly 2 minutes. Stir in flour; cook and stir over low heat 3 minutes. Remove from heat; stir in milk. Return to heat; simmer slowly until thickened, 10 to 15 minutes, stirring occasionally. Stir in cream, 1 tablespoon at a time, until sauce has thinned to desired consistency. Salt and pepper to taste. Stir in lemon juice.

SHRIMP: Saute onion and mushrooms in chafing dish until tender. Stir in prawns, Bechamel sauce and seasonings. Cook 3 to 5 minutes until prawns are thoroughly cooked. (Do not overcook.) Stir in sour cream; heat thoroughly. Ignite warmed brandy; pour over shrimp and serve immediately.

Trout Pecan

2 Servings

Orion Room, IDS Tower, Minneapolis, Charles Venables

¼ cup flour
½ cup chopped pecans
2 (10 to 12-oz.) boned trout
  Olive oil
2 jalapeño peppers, split
6 tablespoons unsalted butter
2 teaspoons snipped fresh parsley
½ lemon
  Salt and pepper

Combine flour and pecans in blender until pecans are finely chopped. Place on large plate. Roll trout in pecan-flour mixture and press mixture so it adheres to trout. Coat saute pan with olive oil; saute jalapeño peppers 3 minutes. Remove peppers. Saute trout in hot oil 7 minutes; turn and saute 5 minutes or until trout flakes easily with fork. Remove trout and keep warm in oven. Add butter to saute pan; brown. Quickly stir in parsley and lemon juice; pour over trout. Salt and pepper to taste. Serve immediately.

Ham Braised in Wine

16 Servings

This rich sauce is a lovely compliment to the smoky flavor of a country ham.

¼ cup butter
6 carrots, cut into julienne strips
4 stalks celery, cut into julienne strips
3 large onions, sliced
8 lb. cooked ham
3 cups dry Madeira wine

SAUCE

3 tablespoons butter
3 tablespoons flour
¾ cup boiling chicken or beef broth
¼ cup dry Madeira wine
½ cup cream
  Salt and pepper

Heat oven to 350°F. Melt ¼ cup butter in 4-inch-deep baking dish. Place vegetables in dish. Bake at 350°F. for 10 to 15 minutes or until vegetables are just tender. Place ham on top of vegetables. Pour 3 cups wine over ham; cover tightly with foil. Continue baking, basting every 45 minutes. Bake ham 15 to 20 minutes per pound. Transfer ham to warm platter; keep warm. Reserve pan juices; cool quickly and skim off fat.

SAUCE: Melt 3 tablespoons butter in saucepan. Stir in flour; cook 3 to 4 minutes. Stir in boiling broth; continue to cook and stir until thick. Add ½ cup of reserved ham juices and ¼ cup wine. Cook and stir until thick, smooth, and well blended. Simmer sauce for several minutes. Stir in cream; blend well. Salt and pepper to taste. Slice ham and serve with sauce.

Orange-Stuffed Leg of Lamb

4 to 8 Servings

3 to 5-lb. leg of lamb, boned
2 cloves garlic, minced
   Grated peel of 1 orange and 1 lemon
   Juice of 1 orange
¼ cup butter, melted
1 cup water
1 teaspoon fresh thyme or ½ teaspoon dried thyme leaves, crushed
1 (16-oz.) pkg. seasoned stuffing mix (4 cups)
   Salt and pepper

TIP: *Your butcher can easily butterfly the lamb for you.*

Heat oven to 350°F. Fold leg of lamb open; rub with garlic. Sprinkle with citrus peels and orange juice. Combine butter with water and thyme; sprinkle over stuffing mix and toss. Spoon 1 to 2 cups stuffing on half of lamb. Fold other half over stuffing; tie roast tightly. Salt and pepper to taste. Bake at 350°F. for 30 minutes per pound. Baste lamb occasionally with pan juices. Bake remaining stuffing, covered, during last 45 minutes.

Butterflied Leg of Lamb with Minted Hollandaise

4 to 8 Servings

The Cookery, Minneapolis, Sara Monick and Mary Tuttle

Sara Monick and Mary Tuttle are the owners and teachers at The Cookery, a Minneapolis cooking school.

3 to 5-lb. leg of lamb, butterflied, all fat removed

MARINADE

½ cup soy sauce
½ cup dry sherry
¼ cup olive oil
2 tablespoons Dijon mustard
1 teaspoon dried rosemary leaves
1 teaspoon grated fresh gingerroot or ½ teaspoon ground ginger
2 cloves garlic, minced

MINTED HOLLANDAISE SAUCE

3 egg yolks
2 tablespoons lemon juice
2 tablespoons finely chopped fresh mint leaves
¼ teaspoon salt
   Dash hot pepper sauce
¾ cup butter, melted

Place lamb in baking dish.
    MARINADE: Combine all marinade ingredients; pour over lamb. Marinate, covered, at least 3 hours at room temperature or overnight in refrigerator. Heat broiler or grill. Cook 10 to 20 minutes per side or until pink in center.
    SAUCE: Combine all sauce ingredients except butter in blender. Blend on high speed 30 seconds. Slowly pour hot melted butter into blender; blend on high speed until slightly thickened. Serve immediately with cooked lamb.

Pork Loin Roast with Orange Barbecue Sauce

8 to 10 Servings

BARBECUE SAUCE

1   (6-oz.) can frozen orange juice concentrate
¼   cup wine vinegar
2   tablespoons brown sugar
2   tablespoons honey
2   teaspoons prepared mustard
2   teaspoons soy sauce

3   to 5-lb. boneless pork rib roast
    Garlic salt

TIP: *To prepare pork roast in oven, heat oven to 325°F. Insert thermometer in roast; place roast in 13 x 9-inch pan, fat side up. Roast at 325°F. for 30 to 40 minutes per pound or until thermometer reaches 170°F.*

Heat barbecue grill. Combine sauce ingredients in medium saucepan; cook over low heat until well blended. Sprinkle roast with garlic salt; insert meat thermometer. Place roast, fat side up, directly on hot grill. Grill 30 minutes. Baste with barbecue sauce. Continue grilling until thermometer reaches 170°F., basting every 20 to 30 minutes. Remove from grill and allow to stand 5 to 10 minutes before slicing. Heat any remaining sauce; serve with roast.

Plum-Glazed Ham

10 to 12 Servings

5   to 7-lb. precooked ham
    Whole cloves

GLAZE

¼   cup chutney
¼   cup plum jam
1   teaspoon rice wine vinegar
⅛   teaspoon hot pepper sauce
1   tablespoon Dijon mustard
1   clove garlic, minced
½   cup packed brown sugar

Remove rind and excess fat from ham. Score remaining layer of fat in diamond pattern; stud with cloves. Place ham on rack in roasting pan. Bake at 325°F. 18 to 24 minutes per pound.
  GLAZE: Heat all glaze ingredients in saucepan. One hour before ham is done, spread glaze over surface; continue baking.

Baked Ham with Peach Sauce

3   to 5-lb. boneless cooked ham

PEACH SAUCE

1   cup sugar
2   tablespoons cornstarch
2   teaspoons seasoned salt
2   teaspoons dry mustard
½   teaspoon paprika
1   cup cold water
⅓   cup orange juice
¼   cup vinegar
2   egg yolks, beaten
1½   cups sliced fresh peaches (or frozen peaches, thawed and drained)

Heat oven to 325°F. Place ham in baking pan. Bake at 325°F. for 15 to 20 minutes per pound.
   SAUCE: Combine sugar, cornstarch, seasonings, water, orange juice and vinegar in 1½-quart saucepan. Heat, stirring constantly, until thickened; remove from heat. Stir small amount of mixture into egg yolks; mix well. Stir egg mixture back into sauce and heat about 1 minute; do not boil. Just before serving, stir in peaches; heat through. Serve with ham.

TIP: *Sauce can be prepared ahead; cover with plastic wrap or waxed paper to prevent a film from forming on top. Stir in peaches just before serving.*

Gingered Pork and Scallions

6 Servings

Serve with fried or white rice.

1½   lb. pork tenderloin
2   teaspoons grated fresh gingerroot
1   teaspoon crumbled dried red peppers
2   cloves garlic, minced
2   tablespoons peanut oil
1½   teaspoons sesame oil
1½   cups chicken broth
2¼   cups scallions, including tops, cut into strips
2½   tablespoons cornstarch
⅓   cup water
¼   cup soy sauce

Partially freeze meat; slice into thin strips. Sprinkle with gingerroot and red peppers. In large skillet, brown meat and garlic in oils. Add chicken broth; simmer, covered, 5 minutes. Add scallions; simmer, covered, 5 minutes. Combine cornstarch, water and soy sauce; add to skillet. Cook and stir over medium heat until mixture thickens, about 3 minutes.

TIP: *Shitake mushrooms (½ cup, drained) are a wonderful addition. Add with scallions.*

Pork Tenderloin Wrap-Ups

6 Servings

These flavor combinations are unique. An especially colorful entree.

5	medium sweet potatoes
½	cup packed brown sugar
3	tablespoons butter
12	slices bacon
6	pork tenderloin slices
	Salt, pepper, and garlic salt to taste
6	slices fresh or canned pineapple

Trim woody parts from sweet potatoes. Wash and cook, covered, in boiling salted water to cover 30 to 40 minutes. Drain, peel and mash. (Should make 3 cups.) Season with brown sugar and butter. Heat oven to 350°F. Crisscross 2 slices bacon on flat surface. Place pork tenderloin on top of bacon slices; season with salt, pepper and garlic salt. Place pineapple slice on tenderloin. Place ½ cup sweet potatoes on pineapple. Wrap bacon up around meat, pineapple and sweet potato; fasten with toothpick. Repeat with remaining tenderloins; place in deep baking dish. Cover tightly with foil. Bake at 350°F. for 1¼ hours. Remove foil for final 20 minutes to allow bacon to brown.

TIP: *Tenderloins can be assembled and refrigerated until ready to bake.*

Pork Tenderloin with Sesame Stuffing

6 Servings

2	(1-lb.) pork tenderloins
1	beef-flavor bouillon cube
¼	cup boiling water
¼	cup chopped celery
2	tablespoons minced onion
¼	cup butter or margarine
¼	cup sesame seeds, lightly toasted
2	cups coarse fresh bread crumbs
1	egg, slightly beaten
½	to 1 teaspoon poultry seasoning
4	to 6 slices bacon
½	to 1 teaspoon salt
⅛	teaspoon pepper

Butterfly tenderloins by slicing lengthwise but not cutting completely through. Open each tenderloin to make flat piece. Dissolve bouillon cube in boiling water. Sauté celery and onion in butter in medium saucepan until transparent. Add bouillon, sesame seeds, crumbs, egg and poultry seasoning; toss to mix. Spoon stuffing onto cut side of 1 tenderloin; place second tenderloin on top, cut side down. Cover with bacon. Wrap string around and tie to hold tenderloins together. Sprinkle with salt and pepper; place on rack in shallow roasting pan. Heat oven to 350°F. Bake about 1 hour or until pork is done.

Fillets Madeira

6 Servings

3 tablespoons butter or margarine
8 oz. fresh mushrooms, sliced
2 tablespoons flour
1 teaspoon salt
¼ teaspoon freshly ground pepper
1 cup whipping cream
⅓ cup Madeira wine
3 tablespoons butter or margarine
6 beef fillets, ¾-inch thick
  Salt and pepper
1 tablespoon snipped fresh parsley

Melt 3 tablespoons butter in skillet; add mushrooms and saute 5 minutes. Stir in flour, 1 teaspoon salt and ¼ teaspoon pepper. Stir in cream; cook over low heat 5 minutes. Stir in wine; keep warm over low heat. In separate skillet melt 3 tablespoons butter; saute fillets about 4 minutes per side. Salt and pepper if desired. Place fillets on serving platter; pour sauce over fillets. Sprinkle with parsley.

Malayan Tenderloin Tips

4 Servings

2 cups Bechamel Sauce with Curry (page 139)
1 to 1½ lb. choice beef tenderloin tips
½ cup butter or margarine
½ cup finely chopped onion
4 oz. fresh mushrooms, sliced
  Dash salt
  Dash pepper
  Dash Maggi seasoning
1 bottle Escoffier sauce Diable
½ cup Burgundy wine
½ cup brandy, warmed

Prepare Bechamel sauce. Cut tenderloin tips into julienne strips. Melt butter in chafing dish over low heat. Add onion and mushrooms; saute until tender. Stir in tenderloin tips; season with salt, pepper and Maggi seasoning. Stir in prepared Bechamel sauce, sauce Diable and wine; heat 2 minutes. Flame with brandy and serve immediately.

Individual Beef Wellingtons

4 Servings

Easy and elegant.

4 (4-oz.) beef tenderloin fillets
1 clove garlic, minced
  Salt and pepper
2 tablespoons butter or margarine

FILLING

8 oz. fresh mushrooms, finely chopped
¼ cup chopped onion
¼ cup dry sherry
2 tablespoons snipped fresh parsley

CRUST

4 frozen unbaked patty shells, thawed
1 egg, beaten

WINE SAUCE

2 tablespoons butter or margarine
⅓ cup chopped onion
6 fresh mushrooms, sliced
2 tablespoons flour
½ cup dry red wine
1 (10½-oz.) can beef broth
1 bay leaf
¼ teaspoon salt
¼ teaspoon Worcestershire sauce
  Dash pepper

Heat oven to 425°F. Grease 15 x 10-inch jelly roll pan. Rub fillets with garlic, salt and pepper to taste. Saute fillets in 2 tablespoons butter, 2 to 4 minutes per side. Reserve pan drippings for filling. Drain fillets on paper towels. Refrigerate.

FILLING: Add chopped mushrooms, ¼ cup onion, sherry and parsley to pan drippings. Cook and stir until onion is tender and all liquid is absorbed. Spread equal portions of filling over top of each chilled steak. Refrigerate while preparing crust.

CRUST: Roll out each patty shell into 6-inch square on lightly floured surface. Place fillets, mushroom side down, on crusts. Fold dough over meat, enclosing it completely; seal edges with beaten egg. Place seam side down in prepared pan. Brush all over with beaten egg. Bake at 425°F. for 15 to 20 minutes or until crust is golden. Meanwhile prepare wine sauce.

SAUCE: Melt 2 tablespoons butter over medium heat. Saute ⅓ cup onion and sliced mushrooms in butter; stir in flour. Gradually stir in wine and broth; add bay leaf and stir until sauce thickens. Season with salt, Worcestershire sauce and pepper. Reduce heat to low; simmer 10 minutes. Remove bay leaf. Serve sauce over fillets.

TIP: *Fillets can be prepared ahead and refrigerated until ready to bake.*

Party Tacos

8 to 10 Servings

Serve this as a "Do it Yourself" buffet; have guests layer their own plates. Excellent for a crowd!

<u>MEAT SAUCE</u>

2 lb. ground beef
1 large onion, chopped
1 (8-oz.) can tomato sauce
1 (6-oz.) can tomato paste
2 cups water
2 tablespoons sugar
2 cloves garlic, minced
1 teaspoon dried oregano leaves, crushed
1 teaspoon chili powder
1 teaspoon salt
1 teaspoon ground cumin
1 cup cooked rice
1 (15-oz.) can pinto beans, undrained

<u>DRESSING</u>

1 (8-oz.) pkg. cream cheese, softened
2 cups mayonnaise
2 cups buttermilk
1 teaspoon pepper
1 teaspoon salt
1 teaspoon onion salt
1 teaspoon garlic powder

1 (24-oz. pkg.) regular size corn chips
8 oz. (2 cups) shredded Cheddar cheese
1 bunch green onions, including tops, chopped
1 head iceberg lettuce, shredded
4 tomatoes, seeded and chopped
2 (4¼-oz.) cans sliced ripe olives, drained
2 to 3 ripe avocados, peeled, pitted and sliced

<u>MEAT SAUCE</u>: Brown ground beef and onion in skillet; drain. Stir in remaining meat sauce ingredients except rice and beans; simmer at least 40 minutes. Stir in rice and undrained beans; simmer 5 minutes longer.

<u>DRESSING</u>: Combine all dressing ingredients in blender; mix well. To assemble tacos, layer on individual plates as follows: corn chips, hot meat sauce, shredded cheese, green onions, lettuce, tomatoes, olives and avocados; top with dressing.

Veal Paprika

3   lb. veal steak, cut into 2-inch pieces and pounded
1   cup all-purpose flour
4   teaspoons paprika
1   to 2 teaspoons salt
2   teaspoons pepper
1   cup butter or margarine
2   cloves garlic, halved
1   (10½-oz.) can beef consommé (not broth)
2   cups dairy sour cream
1   teaspoon dried basil leaves, crushed
⅛   teaspoon dried rosemary leaves, crushed
1   teaspoon lemon juice
½   cup Burgundy wine
8   oz. fresh mushrooms, sliced

Dredge veal in mixture of flour, paprika, salt and pepper; reserve flour mixture. Melt butter in skillet with garlic pieces. Add veal and brown well. Remove garlic and veal. Place veal in 2½-quart casserole. Brown mushrooms in skillet; set aside. Combine remaining flour mixture, consommé, sour cream, basil, rosemary, lemon juice and wine; stir in mushrooms. Pour over veal. Cover; refrigerate 8 hours or overnight. Heat oven to 350°F. Bake, covered, for 45 minutes. Serve with wild rice or noodles, if desired.

TIP: *Chicken breast or pork tenderloin can be substituted for veal.*

Garlic Pepper Steak

MARINADE

¼   cup vegetable oil
2   tablespoons lemon juice
2   tablespoons soy sauce
2   tablespoons chopped green onions
2   cloves garlic, minced
1   teaspoon coarsely ground pepper
1   teaspoon celery salt

1½   to 2 lb. lean flank steak

MARINADE: Combine all marinade ingredients; pour over steak. Cover; refrigerate 8 hours or overnight.

Heat broiler or barbecue grill. Remove meat from marinade; broil or grill 3 to 4 inches from heat for 3 to 5 minutes per side or until cooked, but pink in center. Slice meat on a diagonal.

Beef Tenderloin with Mustard Tarragon Sauce

4 to 6 Servings

Cornichons, small sour French pickles, are also delicious on cheese and pâté platters. Found in the gourmet food section.

3 tablespoons unsalted butter, softened
2 tablespoons Dijon mustard
2 lb. beef tenderloin, at room temperature
2 tablespoons vegetable oil
   Salt and pepper
¼ cup minced shallots
1 cup dry white wine
1½ tablespoons minced fresh tarragon (or 2 teaspoons dried tarragon leaves)
1 tablespoon whipping cream
8 cornichons, cut into julienne strips, if desired
   Salt and pepper, if desired

Heat oven to 550 °F. Cream butter and mustard in small bowl; cover and refrigerate. Rub meat with oil; salt and pepper to taste. Place meat in shallow roasting pan; roast at 550 °F. for 23 minutes for medium rare. Remove to platter; cover loosely with foil. Let stand 15 minutes. Combine shallots, wine and tarragon in saucepan. Cook over medium-high heat until wine is reduced to 3 tablespoons. (This can be done ahead, refrigerated and reheated.) Stir in cream and cornichons; cook over low heat. Gradually whisk in chilled mustard butter and any extra meat juice from platter. Do not boil sauce after adding cream. Salt and pepper to taste. Slice meat and serve with sauce.

Rouladen

*6 Servings
(2 to 3 Rolls per Serving)*

12 to 18 slices thin top beef round steak
12 to 18 teaspoons Dijon mustard
   Freshly ground black pepper
6 to 9 slices bacon, halved
1 or 2 onions, cut into 12 to 18 wedges
2 tablespoons vegetable oil
1½ cups beef bouillon
1½ cups dry red wine
   Flour
   Kitchen Bouquet, if desired

Spread each steak slice with mustard; sprinkle with pepper and top with 1 piece of bacon. Place onion wedge at one end and roll up; secure with toothpick. Brown rolls in oil in skillet; drain. Add bouillon and wine; cover and simmer 2½ to 3 hours. Remove rolls to heated platter. Thicken sauce with a little flour; darken with Kitchen Bouquet.

Veal Pistachio

6 Servings

1 lb. (¼-inch) veal scallops, lightly pounded
  Flour
2 tablespoons vegetable oil
½ cup Madeira (or Marsala) wine
1 cup whipping cream
1¼ cups thinly sliced fresh mushrooms
2½ oz. prosciutto ham, diced
30 to 45 natural pistachio nuts
  Freshly ground pepper
  Snipped fresh parsley

Dredge veal lightly in flour. Heat oil in large skillet over medium-high heat. Cook veal about 1 minute per side or until tender. Transfer to heated platter; cover with foil. Drain oil from skillet; add Madeira to skillet and heat to boiling. Boil until reduced by half. Add cream, mushrooms, prosciutto and pistachios; boil until liquid is reduced by half, coating back of spoon. Pepper to taste. Pour sauce over veal; serve immediately. Garnish with snipped parsley.

Veal with Sorrel Sauce

4 Servings

BEURRE MANIE

2 tablespoons butter
2 tablespoons flour

¼ cup butter
4 veal chops
  Salt and freshly ground black pepper
2 tablespoons chopped carrot
2 tablespoons chopped shallots
1 cup dry white wine
2 tablespoons liquid beef broth
1 cup whipping cream
1 cup finely shredded sorrel leaves
1 slice prosciutto ham, ⅛ inch thick, cut into julienne strips, if desired

BEURRE MANIE: Knead 2 tablespoons butter and 2 tablespoons flour together until blended; shape into small balls. Refrigerate.

  Heat ¼ cup butter in heavy skillet just large enough to hold chops in single layer. Salt and pepper chops to taste. Saute in butter over medium heat until well browned on both sides. (Do not allow butter to burn.) Reduce heat to low; simmer, covered, 15 minutes or until tender. Transfer chops to warm platter. Add carrot, shallots, wine and beef broth to drippings in skillet. Cook, stirring over high heat until liquid is reduced by half. Stir in cream; cook, stirring until reduced by half. Stir in sorrel, half of beurre manie and any juices remaining on platter of chops. (If sauce is too thin, add remaining beurre manie and cook until sauce is of medium consistency.) Spoon sauce over chops. Sprinkle with prosciutto.

TIP: *Fresh sorrel leaves can be purchased in the product department with other fresh herbs.*

Veal Capri

4 Servings

1½ lb. veal scallops
3 tablespoons flour
Salt and pepper
3 tablespoons olive oil
1 tablespoon butter or margarine
2 tablespoons brandy, warmed
2 tablespoons chopped onion
4 oz. fresh mushrooms, sliced
2 tablespoons amaretto
2 tablespoons brown stock
1½ tablespoons cream
1 tablespoon snipped fresh parsley

Dredge veal in mixture of flour, salt and pepper. Brown veal quickly in oil and butter. (Do not overcook.) Carefully ignite brandy and pour over veal. When flame dies down, remove veal to heated platter; keep warm. Saute onion until translucent. Stir in mushrooms and amaretto; reduce liquid by half. Stir in brown stock and cream; pour sauce over veal. Sprinkle with snipped parsley.

Veal with Mustard-Herb Butter

6 Servings

Mustard-Herb Butter is also great on steak.

MUSTARD-HERB BUTTER

6 tablespoons unsalted butter, softened
2 tablespoons Dijon mustard
1 shallot, minced
2 tablespoons snipped Italian parsley
2 tablespoons snipped chives
Black pepper

VEAL

6 (4-oz.) veal cutlets
¼ cup light olive oil
Salt and pepper
6 lemon slices

BUTTER: Combine butter and mustard; blend in shallot, parsley, chives and pepper.
VEAL: Prepare medium-hot fire in barbecue grill. Trim off any connective tissue and tendons; pound veal between lightly oiled parchment paper until about ¼ inch thick. Lightly oil cutlets again; salt and pepper to taste. Grill cutlets 20 seconds; turn a quarter turn. Grill 20 seconds longer; baste with olive oil; turn over. Grill 20 seconds; turn a quarter turn. Total cooking time: 1½ minutes. Place 1 tablespoon mustard butter on each cutlet. Garnish with lemon slices. (Can also be prepared in skillet on stove.)

Cannelloni

6 Servings

An old Italian family recipe.

BECHAMEL SAUCE

¼ cup butter
¼ cup flour
1 cup milk
1 cup whipping cream
1 teaspoon salt
⅛ teaspoon white pepper

FILLING

2 tablespoons olive oil
¼ cup finely chopped onion
1 teaspoon finely chopped garlic
1 (10-oz.) pkg. frozen chopped spinach, thawed and squeezed dry
1 lb. lean ground beef
1 tablespoon butter or margarine
5 tablespoons grated Parmesan cheese
2 eggs, lightly beaten
2 tablespoons whipping cream
½ teaspoon dried oregano leaves, crushed
   Salt and pepper
1 (16-oz.) pkg. manicotti (or fresh pasta cut into 4 x 4-inch squares)
2 (8-oz.) cans tomato sauce
   Butter or margarine
   Grated Parmesan cheese

SAUCE: Melt ¼ cup butter in saucepan; stir in flour with whisk. Add milk and 1 cup whipping cream, stirring constantly until sauce thickens and begins to boil. Reduce heat; simmer until sauce coats whisk. Remove from heat; add salt and pepper.

FILLING: Grease 13 x 9-inch baking dish. Heat oil in skillet. Add onions and garlic; cook until soft but not brown. Stir in spinach; cook until moisture has evaporated and spinach sticks slightly to pan. Remove mixture to bowl. Brown meat in 1 tablespoon butter, breaking up lumps. Add meat to spinach mixture. Stir in Parmesan cheese, eggs, 2 tablespoons whipping cream, oregano, salt and pepper; mix well.

Cook noodles in boiling salted water until tender but still firm; drain. Keep noodles in cold water until ready to fill. Heat oven to 375°F. Coat bottom of 13 x 9-inch baking dish with 1 can tomato sauce. Fill noodles with meat mixture; place in baking dish. Pour cream sauce over noodles. Spoon remaining tomato sauce over cream sauce. Dot with butter; sprinkle with Parmesan cheese. Bake at 375°F. for 25 minutes or until heated through.

TIP: *Noodles can be filled, placed in casserole and refrigerated several hours before adding sauce and baking.*

Pasta, Rice and Potatoes

Spiral Primavera

24 Servings

DRESSING

1½ cups Ranch buttermilk dressing (not bottled)
1½ cups combined grated Parmesan and Romano cheeses

SALAD

2 lb. rotini (spiral pasta), cooked, drained and cooled
1 (8-oz.) bottle Italian dressing
4 carrots, cut into ¼-inch slices
1 head cauliflower, broken into florets
2 lb. broccoli, broken into florets
4 small zucchini, cut into ¼-inch slices
2 celery stalks, cut into ¼-inch slices
1 large bunch scallions, sliced
2 cups sliced fresh mushrooms
   Dried or fresh tarragon leaves, to taste
   Salt and pepper to taste

DRESSING: Combine buttermilk dressing and cheeses; set aside.
  SALAD: Toss rotini with enough Italian dressing to coat well; refrigerate 2 hours. Blanch carrots, cauliflower, broccoli, zucchini and celery. Drain excess Italian dressing from rotini. Combine with vegetables in large bowl. Toss with dressing. Season with tarragon, salt and pepper. Refrigerate until serving time.

Italian Herb Chicken

10 Servings

Rosebud Grocery, Edina and Minnetonka, Joan Donatelle

2 lb. fresh egg fusilli, cooked, drained and cooled
   Olive oil
2 lb. boneless chicken breast, cubed
2 medium zucchini, sliced
1 red bell pepper, cut into strips
1 (3½-oz.) jar pickled cocktail onions
2 cups Pesto Sauce (page 64)
1 cup Red Wine Vinaigrette (page 87)
   Salt and freshly ground pepper

Place fusilli in large bowl; toss with small amount of olive oil. Saute chicken in small amount of olive oil until cooked through. Add chicken, vegetables, Pesto Sauce and Red Wine Vinaigrette to fusilli; toss. Salt and pepper to taste. Refrigerate.

Vegetable Fettuccine Carbonara

6 to 8 Servings

A creamy bacon-and-egg pasta dish with vegetables. Serve it for brunch!

4   eggs
¼   cup whipping cream
8   slices bacon, chopped
1   cup sliced fresh mushrooms
1   cup sliced carrots
1   cup sliced zucchini
½   cup cauliflower florets
½   cup sliced scallions
1   red bell pepper, cut into strips
1   clove garlic, minced
1   (1-lb.) pkg. uncooked fettuccine
¼   cup butter, cut into pieces
1   cup grated Parmesan cheese
    Salt and freshly ground pepper

Beat eggs with cream in small bowl; set aside. Fry bacon in large skillet until crisp; remove with slotted spoon and set aside. Add vegetables and garlic to skillet; saute 5 to 7 minutes or until tender-crisp. Cook fettuccini as directed on package; drain well. Transfer to large serving bowl. Add butter and toss. Add egg mixture; toss lightly. Add vegetables, bacon and cheese; toss again. Salt and pepper to taste. Serve hot.

Pasta Estivi

2 to 4 Servings

Great as a first course. Add Greek olives for variation. Serve in summer with home grown tomatoes!

3   large tomatoes, peeled and cut into 1-inch pieces
1   red onion, sliced and separated into rings
5   tablespoons olive oil
1½ tablespoons white wine vinegar
¼   cup snipped fresh basil leaves (or 2 tablespoons dried basil)
    Freshly ground pepper
12 oz. uncooked spinach noodles
⅓   cup grated Parmesan cheese

Combine tomatoes, onion, oil, vinegar and basil. Sprinkle with pepper; let stand at least 1 hour. Cook noodles as directed on package; drain. Spoon tomato mixture over hot noodles; toss with Parmesan cheese.

Fettuccine with Fresh Herbs, Salmon and Scallops

6 Servings

Murray's, Minneapolis, Ronald G. Procenko

Murray's Restaurant, a Minneapolis landmark is famous for its butter-knife steak and seafood.

1	lb. fettuccine, cooked, drained and cooled
2	tablespoons olive oil
2½	cups water
	Juice of 1 lemon
6	(4-inch) parsley stems
6	(4-inch) rosemary stems
6	(4-inch) scallion tops
6	whole allspice
1½	cups fresh scallops
2	cups fresh boneless salmon

SAUCE

¼	cup butter or margarine
1	tablespoon minced garlic
1	tablespoon minced scallion, white part only
2	cups whipping cream
½	teaspoon salt
	Dash nutmeg
¼	cup chopped fresh dill
¼	cup chopped fresh basil
2	tablespoons snipped fresh rosemary
6	tablespoons grated Parmesan cheese
1	teaspoon freshly ground black pepper
1	cup pine nuts, toasted
½	cup chopped fresh parsley

Toss fettuccine with olive oil; refrigerate. Combine 2½ cups water, lemon juice, parsley, rosemary, scallion tops and allspice in medium saucepan. Heat to boiling; add scallops and poach 2 to 3 minutes. Remove scallops; drain well. Add salmon; poach 4 minutes. Remove salmon; drain well.

SAUCE: Melt butter in large skillet; saute garlic and scallions 1 minute over low heat. Add cream, salt, nutmeg and herbs. Cook until reduced by ⅓. Add cheese and mix well; cook 30 seconds. Add fettuccine and cook until thoroughly heated. Add salmon, scallops and pepper; toss lightly until mixed thoroughly. Cook 30 seconds or until hot. Serve on a platter; garnish with pine nuts and parsley.

Spicy Sesame Chicken

12 Servings

*Lightly Epicurean, Excelsior,
Kathleen M. Lightly*

*Very spicy! Vary amount of
red pepper flakes to taste.*

DRESSING

1½ cups soy sauce
¾ cup sesame oil
1½ tablespoons sugar
1 teaspoon ground ginger
3 tablespoons rice wine vinegar
⅓ cup creamy peanut butter
1 tablespoon crushed red pepper flakes

4 cups carrots, cut into julienne strips ¼ x 2-inches, cooked to
      tender-crisp
1 cup thinly sliced green onions
¾ cup sesame seeds, toasted
4 cups shredded cooked chicken
1 lb. vermicelli, cooked, drained and cooled
2 cups fresh snow peas, strings removed

TIP: *For hot entrée combine
pea pods with chicken mixture. Heat in microwave or
double boiler.*

DRESSING: Combine all dressing ingredients in large bowl; mix well. Let
stand 5 minutes.
   Add carrots, onions, sesame seeds and chicken. Toss vermicelli with
vegetable mixture; refrigerate 1 hour or overnight. Garnish with snow peas.

Rainbow Rotini with Shrimp and Peppers

4 to 6 Servings

*Watch the peppers closely to
prevent burning.*

2 large red bell peppers
2 large green bell peppers
¾ lb. egg, spinach and tomato rotini (spiral pasta), cooked, drained and
      cooled
   Salt and pepper
1 lb. medium large shrimp, cooked, peeled and deveined

DRESSING

½ cup white wine vinegar
1 tablespoon Dijon mustard
   Salt and pepper
½ cup olive oil
3 tablespoons snipped fresh basil leaves

Roast peppers in broiler, turning until skins blacken, 10 to 20 minutes.
Wrap in plastic bags and let stand to steam 10 minutes. Remove skins and
seeds. Rinse peppers and pat dry; cut into strips. Place rotini in large bowl;
salt and pepper to taste. Add cooked shrimp and pepper strips.
DRESSING: Blend vinegar, mustard, salt, pepper, oil and basil in food
processor or blender until finely mixed. Toss with rotini, shrimp and peppers. Let stand at room temperature before serving.

Tortellini Baronessa

6 to 8 Servings

Figlio A Restaurant and Bar, Minneapolis, Ned Windnagel

Figlio Restaurant is a popular bistro in Minneapolis.

This pasta makes a great late night supper.

SAUCE

3 cups whipping cream, at room temperature
1 egg yolk, at room temperature
1 lb. grated Parmesan cheese
  Salt and white pepper
  Dash nutmeg

2 lb. uncooked fresh or frozen meat and cheese-filled egg tortellini
4 oz. fresh mushrooms, sauteed
1 cup fresh or frozen peas
4 oz. prosciutto ham, cut into julienne strips

SAUCE: Pour cream into hot saucepan; heat to boiling. Add small amount of hot cream to egg yolk in small bowl; whisk. Return to cream in saucepan. Reduce heat to simmer; add Parmesan cheese, a little at a time, whisking constantly until sauce is thick enough to coat a spoon. Season to taste with salt, pepper and nutmeg; remove from heat.

Cook tortellini as directed on package; drain. Stir tortellini into cream sauce; stir in mushrooms, peas and prosciutto. Heat thoroughly.

Pasta with Ricotta, Eggplant and Basil

2 Servings

Lucia's, Minneapolis, Teri Parsley Starnes

  Salt
1 cup cubed eggplant
8 oz. uncooked rotini (spiral pasta)
10 pimiento pieces, cut into julienne strips
2 cloves garlic
1 to 2 tablespoons olive oil
  Olive oil
  Pinch red pepper flakes
⅔ cup ricotta cheese
2 tablespoons fresh basil leaves, cut into julienne strips
  Salt and pepper
2 tablespoons pine nuts or chopped walnuts
  Grated Parmesan cheese

Sprinkle salt over eggplant; let stand 30 minutes. Rinse eggplant; drain and set aside. Cook rotini as directed on package: rinse, drain and keep warm. Marinate pimiento with garlic in 1 to 2 tablespoons olive oil. Saute eggplant in olive oil over medium high heat 3 to 4 minutes. Add garlic and pimiento mixture with red pepper flakes; cook 1 to 2 minutes longer. Add ricotta cheese; shake pan to mix. Add basil, salt, pepper and pasta; toss until coated. Transfer to serving plate; sprinkle with nuts and Parmesan cheese. Serve immediately.

Crab Fettuccine with Basil Cream Sauce

6 to 8 Servings

This cannot be made ahead but it is so extraordinary that it must be tried. It is a lovely first course.

3   tablespoons butter
3   tablespoons olive oil
2   tomatoes, peeled, seeded and chopped
1   clove garlic, minced
⅓   cup whipping cream
⅓   to ½ cup dry white wine
½   cup finely chopped fresh basil leaves
½   cup cooked fresh or frozen crabmeat
    Salt and pepper
¼   cup grated Parmesan cheese
¼   cup snipped fresh parsley
1   lb. uncooked fresh fettuccine

Melt butter and oil in saucepan over medium heat. Add tomatoes and garlic; simmer slowly until tomatoes soften and begin to break down. Add cream and ⅓ cup white wine. Simmer 10 minutes, thinning with additional wine if sauce becomes thicker than heavy cream. Stir in basil, crabmeat, salt and pepper; simmer 3 minutes. Add ½ of Parmesan cheese and ½ of parsley. Keep sauce warm. Cook pasta as directed on package; drain. Serve with sauce. Garnish with whole basil leaves, remaining cheese and parsley.

Ziti with Prosciutto and Sage Sauce

6 Servings

3   medium cloves garlic
¼   cup olive oil
8   oz. thinly sliced prosciutto ham, cut into fine strips
⅔   cup chopped walnuts
1   lb. uncooked ziti or similar short tubular pasta
¼   cup unsalted butter, melted
1   cup grated Parmesan cheese
30 fresh sage leaves, coarsely chopped
½   teaspoon coarsely cracked pepper
    Salt
    Red bell pepper slices

Saute garlic in olive oil in large skillet until golden. Remove garlic and discard. Add prosciutto and walnuts to skillet. Cook over low heat, stirring occasionally until walnuts are toasted and prosciutto fat is translucent. Remove from heat. Cook pasta in boiling water 12 to 15 minutes; drain. Toss with proscuitto and walnut mixture. Add butter, cheese, sage leaves, pepper and salt to taste; toss again. Garnish with red pepper slices.

Spicy Sesame Noodles

10 Servings

Rosebud Grocery, Edina and Minnetonka, Joan Donatelle

2   lb. fresh buckwheat spaghetti, cooked, drained and cooled
    Olive oil
3   medium carrots, shredded
1   bunch scallions, chopped

DRESSING

¼   cup sesame seeds
1   tablespoon vegetable oil
    Pinch red pepper flakes
¼   teaspoon cayenne pepper
2   cloves garlic, minced
1   tablespoon grated fresh gingerroot
½   cup rice vinegar
¼   cup sesame oil
¼   cup vegetable oil
2   tablespoons soy sauce

Place spaghetti in large bowl, toss with small amount of olive oil. Add carrots and scallions; refrigerate.

TIP: *Buckwheat pasta is more fragile than regular pasta and must be handled carefully.*

DRESSING: Saute sesame seeds in 1 tablespoon oil until golden brown. Add red pepper flakes, cayenne, garlic and gingerroot. Continue to saute 1 minute. Remove from heat; add remaining dressing ingredients. Blend well. Toss with spaghetti mixture. Refrigerate.

Apricot and Avocado Rice

12 Servings

¾   cup chopped onion
¼   cup butter or margarine
2   cups uncooked converted rice
4   teaspoons instant chicken bouillon
4   cups hot water
2   to 3 teaspoons curry powder
½   teaspoon garlic salt
2   drops hot pepper sauce
1   cup chopped dried apricots
¼   cup snipped fresh parsley
1   cup slivered almonds, toasted
2   avocados, peeled and diced

Saute onion in butter in large heavy saucepan. Stir in rice, bouillon, water, curry powder, garlic salt, hot pepper sauce and dried apricots; heat to boiling. Reduce heat; simmer until liquid is absorbed, 20 to 25 minutes. Let stand 5 minutes. Stir in parsley and almonds. Garnish with avocados.

Seafood Wild Rice

16 Servings

Lightly Epicurean, Excelsior, Kathleen Lightly

Lightly Epicurean features Minnesota wild rice in this delicious salad.

DRESSING

1	tablespoon minced garlic
2	tablespoons curry powder
¼	cup olive oil
2	cups mayonnaise
2	tablespoons sugar
½	cup orange juice
¼	cup lemon juice
¼	cup chopped chutney
½	teaspoon black pepper

WILD RICE

1	lb. uncooked wild rice
5	cups chicken stock or broth
1½	cups frozen petite peas
¾	cup diced celery
½	cup chopped green onion
1	lb. small or medium shrimp, cooked, peeled and deveined
1	lb. sea legs or crabmeat, cut into ½-inch pieces

DRESSING: Saute garlic and curry in olive oil in small skillet. (Watch carefully so it doesn't burn.) Combine remaining dressing ingredients in medium bowl; mix well. Add garlic mixture and whisk thoroughly.

WILD RICE: Simmer rice in chicken stock 1 hour, until rice is tender and has puffed open. Drain and cool. Add remaining ingredients; toss with dressing.

Pasta with Italian Sausage

4 Servings

TIP: *This is a very versatile recipe: Ham, poultry or seafood can be substituted for sausage. Zucchini, pea pods or asparagus can be substituted for mushrooms. Fresh fennel, oregano or cilantro can also be added.*

1	lb. bulk mild Italian sausage
1	lb. fresh mushrooms, sliced
1	lb. uncooked fresh spinach fettuccine
1½	cups grated Parmesan cheese
¼	cup snipped fresh basil leaves
	Salt and pepper
3	cups whipping cream
2	tablespoons sherry

Brown sausage and saute mushrooms in skillet; drain. Cook pasta as directed on package; drain and rinse. Place pasta in large saucepan. Add remaining ingredients. Cook over low heat, stirring constantly until thoroughly heated. Serve immediately.

Rice with Raisins and Pine Nuts

4 Servings

1 tablespoon butter or margarine
3 tablespoons minced onion
½ teaspoon minced garlic
1 cup uncooked rice
¼ cup raisins
1½ cups chicken broth
1 tablespoon vegetable oil
¼ cup pine nuts
1 tablespoon butter or margarine

Melt 1 tablespoon butter in saucepan. Add onion and garlic; saute until tender. Stir in rice, raisins and chicken broth. Heat mixture to boiling; cover and simmer 20 to 25 minutes. Heat oil in small skillet; add pine nuts, stirring constantly until toasted and golden brown. Stir toasted pine nuts and 1 tablespoon butter into cooked rice.

Superb Wild Rice

6 to 8 Servings

Easy and delicious!

½ cup uncooked wild rice
½ cup uncooked brown rice
1 cup sliced fresh mushrooms
½ cup chopped onion
3 oz. (¾ cup) shredded Cheddar cheese
1 cup hot chicken broth
2 tablespoons sherry
¼ cup butter or margarine
Salt and pepper to taste

Combine wild and brown rices; soak overnight in water to cover; drain. Heat oven to 350 °F. Combine rices, mushrooms, onion and cheese in 1½-quart casserole. Pour hot broth and sherry over. Dot with butter; salt and pepper to taste. Bake at 350 °F. for 1 hour.

Risotto Milanese

4 Servings

Pronto Ristorante, Minneapolis, Mark Donnay

1   onion, finely chopped
¼   cup butter or margarine
2   cups short grain rice (i.e. Arborio)
4   cups chicken broth
    Pinch of saffron
    Salt to taste
¼   cup grated Parmesan cheese

TIP: *Arborio rice is available at specialty food shops. Its special texture is necessary for the making of risotto.*

Saute onion in butter until tender. Add rice and saute until golden. Slowly add 1 cup of the chicken broth. Continue stirring until broth evaporates, adding more broth slowly to rice until all broth is absorbed. Add saffron with final 2 cups broth. Check for flavor. Add salt if necessary. When done, remove from heat; stir in Parmesan cheese. Serve immediately.

Bulgur Nut Pilaf

4 to 6 Servings

Serve bulgur, a nutty crunchy grain, in place of rice for an unusual taste.

3   tablespoons butter or margarine
1   cup bulgur
2   cups chicken broth
2   medium carrots, shredded
½   teaspoon salt
½   cup finely chopped walnuts
    Shredded carrot and fresh snipped parsley

Heat oven to 350 °F. Melt butter in large ovenproof skillet or saucepan. Saute bulgur in butter about 5 minutes or until lightly browned, stirring occasionally. Stir in broth, 2 shredded carrot and salt. Heat to boiling; cover. Bake at 350 °F. for 25 minutes or until broth is absorbed. Remove from oven; stir in walnuts. Garnish with shredded carrot and snipped parsley.

Wild Rice Casserole

6 Servings

Lola Perpich, First Lady of Minnesota, serves this at the Governor's Residence.

1   cup uncooked wild rice, rinsed
½   cup slivered almonds
2   tablespoons chopped chives or green onions
8   oz. fresh mushrooms, sliced
½   cup butter or margarine
3   cups chicken broth

Heat oven to 325 °F. Combine all ingredients except broth in heavy saucepan. Cook, stirring constantly, until rice turns yellow. Place in 1½-quart casserole; add broth. Cover tightly. Bake at 325 °F. for 1 hour.

Wild Rice with Pecans

6 to 8 Servings

A fresh tasting addition to an elegant salad supper.

1 cup uncooked wild rice
5½ cups chicken broth or stock
1 cup golden raisins
1 cup pecan halves
4 scallions, thinly sliced
  Grated peel of 1 orange
⅓ cup orange juice
¼ cup olive oil
1½ teaspoons salt
  Freshly ground pepper to taste

Place rice in strainer; rinse thoroughly under cold water. Place rice in medium-size heavy saucepan. Add chicken broth; heat to boiling. Reduce heat; simmer uncovered 45 to 60 minutes or until rice is tender. Drain and place in bowl. Add remaining ingredients; toss gently. Let stand at least 2 hours for flavors to develop. Serve at room temperature or heat before serving.

Italian Sage Potatoes

4 to 6 Servings

4 to 6 medium potatoes, unpeeled
1 to 2 cloves garlic, minced
¼ cup olive oil
6 fresh sage leaves, snipped (or 1 tablespoon dried sage, crushed)
  Salt and pepper

Cut potatoes in half lengthwise; cut crosswise into pieces 1-inch wide. Saute garlic in olive oil in large non-stick skillet. Add potatoes and stir to coat with oil. Add sage and salt and pepper to taste. Stir and cover. Reduce heat to low. Cook potatoes 15 to 20 minutes or until tender; tossing occasionally. Remove cover; increase heat to high. Cook potatoes until slightly crisp. Serve hot or at room temperature.

Baked Potatoes with Crab Stuffing

4 Servings

A delicious entrée. Serve with a green salad for a casual supper.

4	large baking potatoes
1	tablespoon butter or margarine
2	large fresh mushrooms, chopped
3	tablespoons whipping cream
3	tablespoons butter or margarine
1	tablespoon grated onion
½	teaspoon salt
¼	teaspoon pepper
1	(6-oz.) can crabmeat, drained and flaked
4	oz. (1 cup) sharp Cheddar cheese, shredded

Bake potatoes at 400°F. for 1 hour and 10 minutes or until very tender when pierced with a knife. Remove potatoes from oven. Reduce oven temperature to 350°F. Melt 1 tablespoon butter in small skillet over moderate heat. Add mushrooms and saute, tossing until tender, about 3 minutes. Cut potatoes in half lengthwise. Scoop out pulp, leaving a shell about ⅛-inch thick. Rice or mash potato until smooth. Heat cream and remaining butter in small saucepan until butter melts; beat into potatoes. Stir in onion, salt, pepper, mushrooms, crabmeat and ⅔ cup cheese. Spoon mixture into potato shells. Sprinkle with remaining ⅓ cup cheese. Place potatoes on cookie sheet. Bake at 350°F. for 20 minutes.

TIP: *Stuffed potatoes can be refrigerated until serving time. Reheat to 350°F. for 30 to 40 minutes.*

Sauteed Potato Casserole

2 to 4 Servings

Nigel's Restaurant, Minneapolis, Tom Williams

For a light supper serve with a green salad tossed with mustard vinaigrette.

½	cup olive oil
2	cloves garlic, minced
4	medium-large red potatoes, peeled and shredded
2	medium zucchini, shredded
2	medium carrots, shredded
2	tablespoons snipped fresh rosemary leaves
2	large tomatoes, diced
	Salt and pepper
4	oz. (1¼ cups) grated Parmesan cheese
½	cup ground hazelnuts or walnuts

Heat broiler. Heat olive oil in 12-inch saute pan until very hot. Carefully add garlic and potatoes to oil. Toss quickly 1 minute. Reduce heat to medium; saute 10 minutes, shaking pan frequently. Add zucchini, carrots and rosemary; saute 3 minutes. Add tomatoes and continue cooking 2 minutes longer. Salt and pepper to taste. Shake pan to mix well. Slide mixture onto ovenproof serving dish. Combine cheese and nuts; sprinkle over potatoes. Broil until browned. Serve immediately.

Swedish Potatoes

8 Servings

6 medium baking potatoes, peeled and thinly sliced
1 teaspoon salt
¼ teaspoon white pepper
½ small onion, chopped
1 egg, lightly beaten
3 oz. (¾ cup) shredded Gruyere cheese
1 cup milk
1 cup whipping cream
2 oz. (½ cup) shredded Gruyere cheese
3 tablespoons butter or margarine

Heat oven to 350 °F. Butter 2-quart casserole. Combine potatoes, salt, pepper, onion, egg and 3 oz. cheese. Heat milk and cream to boiling in saucepan; combine with potato mixture. Place mixture in prepared casserole. Sprinkle with remaining cheese and dot with butter. Bake at 350 °F. for 1 hour. If top is not browned when done, broil until lightly browned.

Sweet Potato-Pear Casserole

8 Servings

8 to 10 medium sweet potatoes
¼ cup butter or margarine, melted
¾ cup maple syrup
½ teaspoon cinnamon
¼ teaspoon nutmeg
1 (29-oz.) can pear halves, drained

Butter shallow casserole. Cook potatoes in boiling salted water until tender; peel and slice. Heat oven to 350 °F. Combine butter, syrup, cinnamon and nutmeg; mix well. Arrange potatoes and pears in prepared casserole. Pour syrup mixture over. Bake at 350 °F. for 30 to 40 minutes.

Vegetables

Zucchini and Cheese Casserole

6 to 8 Servings

A great side dish for Italian entrées.

2 to 3 medium zucchini
1 teaspoon salt
2 tablespoons olive oil
½ cup chopped onion
1 clove garlic, minced
1 (16-oz.) can tomatoes, undrained
½ teaspoon dried basil leaves, crushed
½ teaspoon dried oregano leaves, crushed
¼ teaspoon pepper
2 eggs
3 tablespoons flour
1 cup grated Parmesan cheese
8 oz. (2 cups) shredded Mozzarella cheese

Heat oven to 350°F. Cut unpeeled zucchini into ½-inch thick slices; sprinkle with salt. Spread on waxed paper. Let stand 15 minutes; rinse and drain. Heat 2 tablespoons olive oil in skillet. Saute onion and garlic until tender. Add tomatoes and seasonings; cover and simmer. Combine eggs and flour; beat until smooth. Dip zucchini slices into egg mixture; saute in hot oil until browned on both sides. Place in single layer in 10 x 7-inch baking dish. Cover with ½ of tomato sauce, ½ of Parmesan and ½ of Mozzarella. Repeat layers. Bake, uncovered, at 350°F. for 45 to 60 minutes.

Zucchini and Red Pepper Saute

4 Servings

A colorful accent to a special dinner.

1½ tablespoons butter or margarine
1 tablespoon olive oil
1 small onion, thinly sliced
1 small red bell pepper, cut into julienne strips
½ teaspoon snipped fresh thyme leaves
2 small zucchini, cut into julienne strips

Heat butter and oil in medium skillet; saute onion and red pepper until slightly tender, 3 to 4 minutes. Stir in thyme and zucchini; saute 5 to 6 minutes. Vegetables should be tender-crisp. Serve immediately.

Zippy Carrots

8 to 12 Servings

2   lb. carrots, cut into julienne strips
¾   cup mayonnaise
¼   cup carrot juice
1   tablespoon prepared horseradish
1   tablespoon chopped onion
    Bread crumbs
    Paprika

Cook carrots in water until tender. Heat oven to 350°F. Arrange carrots in 3-quart casserole. Combine mayonnaise, carrot juice, horseradish and onion; pour over carrots. Sprinkle with bread crumbs and paprika. Bake at 350°F. for 20 minutes.

Asparagus Timbales

8 Servings

The 510 Restaurant, Minneapolis, Jay Sparks

This recipe is from The 510 Restaurant, an elegant restaurant near the Guthrie Theatre.

1½ lb. fresh asparagus (or 1 (10-oz.) pkg. frozen asparagus cuts, thawed and drained)
2   shallots, finely chopped
¼   cup unsalted butter
⅛   teaspoon minced garlic
¼   cup chicken stock or broth
¼   cup dry vermouth
2½ cups whipping cream
4   eggs
4   egg yolks
4   oz. fresh spinach, washed and stemmed
⅛   teaspoon cayenne pepper
    Salt

Butter 8 (6-oz.) custard cups with unsalted butter. Cut asparagus into 1-inch pieces. Gently saute shallots in ¼ cup butter in medium saucepan 3 to 5 minutes. Add asparagus and saute 5 minutes. Add garlic and saute 2 minutes. Add chicken stock and vermouth; continue cooking until liquid is reduced by half. Stir in cream; reduce mixture by one-quarter. Remove from heat; cool about 20 minutes. Heat oven to 300°F. Place 2 eggs, 2 egg yolks and half of the asparagus-cream mixture in a 2-quart blender container. Puree with 2 oz. fresh spinach. Add cayenne and salt to taste. Strain through fine mesh sieve into medium bowl. Repeat with remaining mixture and eggs. Check and adjust seasonings. Fill prepared custard cups with asparagus cream. Tap molds lightly to remove excess air bubbles. Place custard cups in a shallow pan of hot water. Cover with foil. Bake at 300°F. for 50 to 75 minutes. Check at 50 minutes for doneness; timbales should be quite firm to the touch. (Do not overcook.) Remove from oven. To remove timbales from custard cups, loosen around inside edge of mold with thin knife blade; invert onto plate. Garnish with melted butter, lemon juice and chopped parsley, if desired.

Zucchini with Pesto and Pine Nuts

6 Servings

Prepare with garden-fresh zucchini and basil; serve with grilled steak.

6   small zucchini, cut into julienne strips
    Salt
2   cups chopped fresh basil leaves
½   cup olive oil
3   tablespoons pine nuts
2   cloves garlic
1   teaspoon salt
1   cup grated Parmesan cheese
2   tablespoons butter or margarine, softened
¼   cup pine nuts
¼   cup unsalted butter

Heat oven to 350°F. Lightly salt zucchini and drain in colander 30 minutes; pat dry with paper towels. Puree basil, olive oil, 3 tablespoons pine nuts, garlic and 1 teaspoon salt in food processor or blender. Transfer to medium bowl; stir in cheese and 2 tablespoons butter; mix well. Toast ¼ cup pine nuts at 350°F. for 10 minutes. Melt unsalted butter in large heavy skillet over medium-high heat. Stir in zucchini; saute until heated through. Add sauce and toasted pine nuts; toss, mixing well.

Tourlou Tava

10 to 12 Servings

Many feel this is a flavorful Greek-style ratatouille — serve with grilled lamb, rice pilaf and Greek salad. Great for buffets.

2   lb. fresh green beans, cut into 1-inch pieces
2   large onions, quartered and sliced
¼   cup snipped fresh dill
½   cup olive oil
4   cloves garlic, chopped
1   cup chopped parsley
1   lb. tomatoes, peeled and chopped
    Salt and pepper to taste
4   to 6 medium zucchini, sliced
2   (10-oz.) pkg. frozen okra, thawed and chopped

Heat oven to 450°F. Combine all ingredients except zucchini and okra in large Dutch oven or casserole. Cover and bake at 450°F. for about 15 minutes or until liquid starts to simmer; reduce oven temperature to 350°F. Bake 45 to 60 minutes. Add zucchini and okra; bake 45 to 60 minutes longer or until all vegetables are tender.

Asparagus and Prosciutto Bundles

6 Servings

A delicious accompaniment to a simple grilled chicken dinner.

30 to 36 spears fresh asparagus
6 slices prosciutto ham
½ cup grated Parmesan cheese
  Freshly ground black pepper
2 cloves garlic, minced
½ cup butter or margarine, melted

Heat oven to 350 °F. Grease 13 x 9-inch baking dish. Steam asparagus until tender-crisp, 4 to 5 minutes. Immediately chill under cold running water. Wrap 5 to 6 asparagus spears in each slice of prosciutto. Place bundles in prepared baking dish. Sprinkle cheese across center of bundles. Season generously with pepper. Combine garlic and melted butter; drizzle over bundles. Bake at 350 °F. for 10 minutes or until cheese is melted and light brown and asparagus is heated through. Remove bundles with slotted spoon; place on heated serving platter.

Broccoli-Cheese Pie

8 Servings

Recipe can be doubled and baked in a 13 x 9-inch casserole for a special buffet presentation.

8 to 10 phyllo sheets
⅔ cup chopped onion
¼ cup butter or margarine
2 (10-oz.) pkg. frozen chopped broccoli, cooked
3 eggs
8 oz. Feta cheese, crumbled
¼ cup snipped fresh parsley
2 tablespoons snipped fresh dill
½ teaspoon salt
¼ teaspoon pepper
½ cup butter or margarine, melted

Heat oven to 350 °F. Thaw phyllo sheets if frozen. Saute onion in ¼ cup butter until golden; add broccoli and saute briefly. Remove from heat. Beat eggs in large bowl; add Feta cheese, parsley, dill, salt, pepper and broccoli-onion mixture; mix well. Brush melted butter on 6 to 8 phyllo sheets. Line 9-inch springform pan with buttered sheets, overlapping edges. Pour filling into pan. Fold overlapping pastry sheets over filling. Cut 2 circles of phyllo dough to fit pan. Brush each circle with butter and place on top of filling. Score top of pie to form 8 wedges. Brush top with remaining butter. Place springform pan on cookie sheet. Bake at 350 °F. for 40 to 50 minutes. Cool 10 minutes. Remove sides of pan and cut into wedges.

Summer Squash with Sun-Dried Tomatoes

6 to 8 Servings

2 tablespoons oil from sun-dried tomatoes
3 to 4 small to medium yellow summer squash, sliced into ¼-inch rounds
6 sun-dried tomatoes, cut into thin strips
4 sprigs fresh rosemary, chopped
  Salt and pepper to taste

Heat oil in small skillet over high heat; saute squash on both sides until light brown. Add tomatoes, rosemary, salt and pepper; toss well. Serve immediately.

Broccoli Puree

4 to 6 Servings

For a colorful presentation serve in hollowed out tomato halves.

1½ lb. broccoli, broken into florets
  Salt and pepper to taste
¼ cup butter or margarine
3 tablespoons flour
3 tablespoons whipping cream
½ to ¾ cup dairy sour cream

Cook broccoli in salted water until just tender, 5 to 10 minutes; drain. Puree in food processor until smooth. Season with salt and pepper. Heat butter in skillet; stir in flour and cook until light brown. Stir in cream; combine mixture with puree. Stir in sour cream; heat thoroughly. Transfer to serving dish. Garnish with broccoli florets, if desired.

Carrots Marguerite

4 Servings

¼ cup butter or margarine
3 green onions (white part only), finely minced
1 lb. carrots, shredded
3 tablespoons honey
½ teaspoon dried thyme leaves, crushed
¼ teaspoon salt
  Dash freshly ground black pepper

Heat butter in large skillet over low heat. Saute onions for a few minutes, just until soft and golden. Stir in carrots, honey, thyme, salt and pepper until carrots are coated. Cover; cook 3 minutes. Serve immediately.

Mediterranean Vegetable Pie

8 Servings

Perfect accompaniment at brunch with your favorite egg dish.

1 medium eggplant, peeled and cut into ¼-inch cubes
1 teaspoon salt
  Pastry for 9-inch 2-crust pie
3 tablespoons grated Parmesan cheese
¾ cup vegetable oil
1 large onion, thinly sliced
1 green pepper, cut into thin strips
1 medium zucchini, thinly sliced
2 cloves garlic, minced
¾ teaspoon dried oregano leaves, crushed
¾ teaspoon dried basil leaves, crushed
½ teaspoon salt
¼ teaspoon pepper
2 medium tomatoes, peeled, seeded and cut into eighths
5 tablespoons grated Parmesan cheese
8 oz. (2 cups) shredded Mozzarella cheese

TIP: Simplify preparation by using refrigerated pie crust.

Place eggplant on paper towels; sprinkle with 1 teaspoon salt, cover with paper towels and weight down with a heavy plate for 30 minutes. Rinse and drain. Heat oven to 425°F. Roll out bottom crust and place in 9-inch pie plate. Sprinkle with 3 tablespoons Parmesan cheese. Heat ½ cup oil in large skillet. Add eggplant; cook, stirring constantly until tender. Place eggplant in large bowl. Heat remaining ¼ cup oil in skillet; add onion, green pepper, zucchini and garlic; cook until vegetables are tender but do not lose their shape. Combine oregano, basil, ½ teaspoon salt and pepper. Place ½ of eggplant in pie shell; add ½ of onion mixture. Arrange ½ of tomato wedges on top. Sprinkle with some herb mixture, 2 tablespoons Parmesan cheese and ½ the mozzarella cheese. Repeat layers with remaining ingredients, reserving 1 tablespoon Parmesan cheese. Roll out top crust; cut into ½-inch strips. Place on vegetables lattice-style; seal and flute edges of pie crust. Brush with milk or water; sprinkle with remaining Parmesan cheese. Bake at 425°F. for 25 minutes or until light brown and bubbling. Cool 15 minutes before cutting.

Squash Puree with Sherry

4 to 6 Servings

1 large butternut squash
¼ cup butter or margarine
2½ tablespoons dry sherry
5 tablespoons butter or margarine, softened
  Salt and pepper to taste

TIP: Prepared squash can be covered and refrigerated. To reheat, place dish in pan of water; cover lightly with parchment paper. Heat at 350°F. for about 20 minutes.

Peel squash; slice into small thin pieces. Melt ¼ cup butter in skillet; saute squash until soft and slightly caramelized, 15 to 20 minutes. Add sherry and toss 2 to 3 minutes. Remove from heat; place squash and remaining butter in food processor or blender. Puree until smooth and fluffy. Transfer to serving dish. Serve immediately.

Artichoke Hearts with Fresh Mint

4 Servings

Wonderful served with roast lamb.

½ cup olive oil
2 (9-oz.) pkg. frozen artichoke hearts
1 medium onion, minced
2 tablespoons sugar
  Salt and pepper
¼ cup white wine vinegar
2 tablespoons water
2 tablespoons minced fresh mint leaves (or 1 teaspoon dried mint leaves)

Heat oil in large stainless steel or enamel skillet over moderately high heat; saute artichoke hearts until golden brown. Add onion and saute the mixture until onion is tender. Sprinkle artichoke hearts with sugar; salt and pepper to taste. Add vinegar and water. Heat to boiling; reduce heat and simmer, stirring occasionally, until artichokes are tender and liquid is syrupy. Transfer mixture to heated serving dish; sprinkle with mint.

Spinach-Artichoke Casserole

8 Servings

2 (10-oz.) pkg. frozen chopped spinach
½ cup chopped onion
¼ cup butter or margarine
2 cups dairy sour cream
½ cup grated Parmesan cheese
  Salt and pepper to taste
1 (16-oz.) can water-packed artichoke hearts, drained
2 tablespoons grated Parmesan cheese

Heat oven to 350 °F. Cook spinach; drain and press dry. Saute onion in butter. Combine sour cream, ½ cup Parmesan cheese, salt and pepper with spinach and onions. Place in 1½-quart casserole. Quarter artichoke hearts and arrange on top of casserole. Sprinkle with 2 tablespoons Parmesan cheese. Bake at 350 °F. for 20 to 30 minutes.

Tomatoes Stuffed with Mushrooms

8 Servings

8 firm tomatoes
½ cup butter or margarine
1¼ lb. fresh mushrooms, sliced
1 cup dairy sour cream
1 tablespoon plus 1 teaspoon flour
3 oz. Roquefort cheese, crumbled
2 tablespoons dry sherry
1 teaspoon snipped fresh parsley
¼ teaspoon dried fines herbes
   Salt and pepper
   Ground blanched almonds
   Paprika

Heat oven to 375°F. Cut slice from top of each tomato. Scoop out pulp. Set tomatoes upside down on paper towels to drain. Melt butter in large skillet; saute mushrooms until all moisture is gone. Combine sour cream with flour; blend into mushrooms; cook and stir until thick and bubbly. Stir in cheese until smooth. Stir in sherry, parsley, fines herbes, salt and pepper; cool. Stuff tomatoes loosely with mushroom filling. Sprinkle tops with almonds and paprika. Bake at 375°F. for 15 minutes or until bubbly. Serve immediately.

Cauliflower, Carrot and Parmesan Quiche

6 to 8 Servings

Great served with a spicy chicken, fish or beef entree.

1 partially baked 9-inch pie shell
1½ cups grated Parmesan cheese
1½ cups coarsely chopped fresh cauliflower, cooked until just tender and drained
1½ cups julienne carrot strips, cooked until just tender and drained
3 eggs
1½ cups whipping cream
   Hot pepper sauce
   Salt and pepper

Heat oven to 300°F. Sprinkle pie shell with half of Parmesan cheese. Arrange cauliflower and carrots evenly over cheese, reserving 10 carrot slices for garnish, if desired. Sprinkle remaining cheese over vegetables. Lightly beat eggs; stir in cream, hot pepper sauce, salt and pepper to taste. Pour egg mixture over vegetables. Arrange reserved carrots in circle on top. Bake at 300°F. about 1 hour, or until top is light brown and filling is set. (Cover pastry edge with foil if necessary to prevent excessive browning.) Let stand at room temperature 15 minutes before serving.

Cauliflower Timbales with Hollandaise Sauce

10 Servings

Pretty when garnished with pimiento slices and fresh parsley.

1½ cups warm cream
4 eggs
¾ teaspoon salt
½ teaspoon paprika
⅛ teaspoon nutmeg
1 tablespoon snipped fresh parsley
1½ cups cooked, drained cauliflower pieces
2 cups Hollandaise Sauce (page 132)

Heat oven to 350 °F. Beat cream, eggs, seasonings and parsley in medium bowl; toss with cauliflower. Pour into 10 individual greased timbale or custard cups, leaving ½ inch space at top. Place in pan with 1 inch of water. Bake at 350 °F. for 40 minutes or until firm. Unmold onto platter; serve with Hollandaise Sauce.

Spaghetti Squash Alfredo

4 Servings

Nigel's, Minneapolis, Tom Williams

Nigel's, Minneapolis — this comfortably upscale restaurant was once an art gallery.

1 large spaghetti squash
2 tablespoons olive oil
4 cloves garlic, minced
4 cups whipping cream
4 oz. (1¼ cups) grated Parmesan cheese
6 oz. cream cheese, cubed
   Salt and freshly grated black pepper

Heat oven to 350 °F. Pierce squash 4 to 6 times with sharp knife. Rub squash with 1 tablespoon olive oil. Place in baking dish; cover with foil. Bake at 350 °F. for 1 to 1½ hours, until tender when pierced with a fork. Remove from oven and cool slightly. Split squash lengthwise with large knife. Scoop out seeds. "Rake" through squash with fork; contents will fall out in strands like spaghetti.
   SAUCE: Heat remaining olive oil in 2-quart saucepan over medium heat. Saute garlic 3 minutes. Add cream and bring to a boil. Reduce heat to simmer; whisk in Parmesan cheese until melted. Stir in cream cheese, one cube at a time. Salt and pepper to taste. Toss squash with sauce; garnish with additional Parmesan cheese, if desired.

Desserts

Raspberry Mousse Meringue Pie

8 to 10 Servings

4 egg whites at room temperature
¼ teaspoon salt
1½ cups sugar
¼ cup sliced almonds
2 (10-oz.) pkg. frozen raspberries, thawed
2 envelopes unflavored gelatin
½ cup amaretto
2 cups whipping cream, whipped
  Fresh raspberries or frozen, thawed and drained

Heat oven to 275°F. Grease 10-inch pie plate. Beat egg whites and salt in large bowl until soft peaks form. Beat in sugar 1 tablespoon at a time until meringue is stiff and glossy. Spread ⅔ of meringue evenly over bottom and sides of pan. Place remaining meringue in pastry bag fitted with large star tip. Pipe meringue rosettes along outer edge of pie plate. Sprinkle meringue with almonds. Bake at 275°F. for 60 minutes or until light brown and very firm to touch. Turn oven off and let meringue cool in oven 2 hours. Purée thawed raspberries in blender or food processor. Press purée through a sieve into a saucepan to remove seeds. Stir in gelatin; cook over low heat, stirring constantly until gelatin is dissolved. Stir in amaretto and chill until syrupy. Fold in whipped cream; chill until mixture mounds when dropped from a spoon. Mound filling in pie shell. Refrigerate until filling is firm. Garnish with fresh raspberries.

Heavenly Blueberry Pie

8 to 10 Servings

1 (10-inch) baked pie crust
1 (8-oz.) pkg. cream cheese, softened
½ cup sugar
½ cup whipping cream
1 teaspoon vanilla or lemon juice
1 cup blueberry jam
1½ cups whipping cream
2 tablespoons powdered sugar
2 cups fresh blueberries

Prepare and bake pie crust. Beat cream cheese, sugar, ½ cup cream and vanilla until thick and smooth. Pour into crust. Spread with jam; refrigerate. Beat 1½ cups whipping cream until soft peaks form. Fold in 2 tablespoons powdered sugar and blueberries. Spread over jam and refrigerate 2 hours or until firm.

Strawberry Imperials

5 egg yolks
½ cup sugar
1½ cups warm milk
3 tablespoons Grand Marnier
1 tablespoon vanilla
1 envelope unflavored gelatin
3 tablespoons cold water
1 cup whipping cream, whipped
2 cups whole fresh strawberries, hulled
4 cups fresh strawberries, sliced
2 tablespoons Kirsch
6 tablespoons red currant jelly
¼ cup sugar

Combine egg yolks and ½ cup sugar in top of double boiler. Beat until mixture is pale yellow. Add warm milk and cook over hot water until mixture coats spoon. Add Grand Marnier and vanilla; pour into large bowl. Sprinkle gelatin over cold water in small saucepan; heat gently until dissolved. Whisk gelatin into egg mixture. Refrigerate, stirring occasionally until mixture begins to mound. Fold whipped cream into egg mixture. Pour into 4 or 6 serving bowls. Top with 2 cups whole strawberries. Refrigerate until serving time. Puree remaining 4 cups strawberries in blender with kirsch, currant jelly and ¼ cup sugar; set aside. To serve, pour sauce over custard.

Rhubarb Strawberry Crumble

4 cups diced rhubarb (½-inch pieces)
1 cup fresh whole strawberries
½ cup sugar
1 cup all-purpose flour
1 cup sugar
1 teaspoon baking powder
¾ teaspoon salt
1 egg, beaten
¾ cup butter or margarine, melted
   Vanilla ice cream or whipped cream, if desired

Heat oven to 350 °F. Combine rhubarb, strawberries and ½ cup sugar. Pour mixture into 9-inch square pan. Combine flour, 1 cup sugar, baking powder, salt and egg in medium bowl. Mix until crumbly. Sprinkle over fruit. Drizzle with melted butter. Bake at 350 °F. for 45 minutes or until browned. Serve with vanilla ice cream or whipped cream.

Strawberry Bavarian Pie

8 to 10 Servings

COCONUT CRUST

⅓ cup butter or margarine, melted
1 (7-oz.) pkg. (2½ cups) flaked coconut

FILLING

1 quart fresh strawberries, sliced
¾ cup sugar
1 envelope unflavored gelatin
½ cup water
2 teaspoons lemon juice
1 cup whipping cream, whipped

CRUST: Heat oven to 300°F. Combine butter and coconut; press into 9-inch pie plate. Bake at 300°F. for 25 to 30 minutes until light brown.

FILLING: Combine strawberries with sugar in large bowl; let stand until sugar dissolves, about 15 to 20 minutes. Sprinkle gelatin over cold water in small saucepan; heat to dissolve. Add gelatin and lemon juice to berries; cool to room temperature. Fold whipped cream into berry mixture. Refrigerate until mixture mounds. Pour into pie shell. Refrigerate 4 hours or until firm.

Mandarin Orange Cake

12 Servings

*Arboretum Tea Room,
Chanhassen, Mary Mueller*

2 cups all-purpose flour
2 cups sugar
2 teaspoons baking soda
1 teaspoon salt
2 cups mandarin orange segments, drained
2 teaspoons vanilla
2 eggs

GLAZE

1½ cups packed brown sugar
6 tablespoons butter
6 tablespoons milk

1 cup whipping cream, whipped and slightly sweetened

Heat oven to 350°F. Grease and flour 13 x 9-inch pan. Combine all cake ingredients in large bowl; beat at medium speed until well blended. Pour into prepared pan. Bake at 350°F. for 35 minutes.

GLAZE: Combine all glaze ingredients in saucepan; heat to boiling. Boil 3 minutes. Poke many small holes in hot cake. Slowly pour hot glaze over cake. Serve topped with whipped cream.

Japanese Fruit Pie

6 to 8 Servings

Unusual and delicious combination.

1 (9-inch) unbaked pie shell

FILLING

1 cup sugar
½ cup flaked coconut
½ cup golden raisins
½ cup chopped pecans
½ teaspoon salt
½ cup butter or margarine, melted
½ teaspoon vanilla
2 eggs, well-beaten

   Whipped cream

Prepare pie shell. Heat oven to 350°F.
   FILLING: Combine all filling ingredients in large bowl. Pour into pie shell. Bake at 350°F. for 40 to 50 minutes or until golden brown. Cool completely. Refrigerate until ready to serve. Serve with whipped cream.

Fruit Tart Valerian

6 to 8 Servings

CRUST

¾ (9½-oz.) box petit beurre or brown edge wafers
6 tablespoons butter or margarine, softened
1 teaspoon vanilla

FILLING

1 cup strawberry jelly
3 tablespoons lemon juice
2 tablespoons Cointreau
2 cups fresh whole strawberries, hulled
1 cup whipping cream, whipped

TIPS: Keep tart at room temperature until ready to garnish with whipped cream (it will get too hard if refrigerated). Serve the same day it is prepared.

Other berries can be substituted for strawberries; use same flavor jelly as berries.

CRUST: Heat oven to 375°F. Combine all crust ingredients in food processor or blender; process until mixed and cookie crumbs are fine. Press into ungreased 10-inch tart pan. Bake at 375°F. for 10 minutes. Cool.
   FILLING: Heat jelly, lemon juice and Cointreau until mixture reaches 220°F. to 225°F. (soft ball stage). Immediately spread filling over cooled crust; arrange berries over top. Cool to room temperature. To serve, remove ring around tart pan. Place tart on serving plate; garnish with whipped cream.

Lemon Mousse with Fresh Raspberry Sauce

8 to 10 Servings

Hint: If you wish to serve more sauce, double the raspberry sauce ingredients.

1 envelope unflavored gelatin
2 tablespoons white wine
⅓ cup lemon juice
1½ tablespoons grated lemon peel
3 eggs, separated
½ cup sugar
1 cup whipping cream, whipped

RASPBERRY SAUCE

1 (10-oz.) pkg. frozen raspberries, thawed and drained
2 to 3 tablespoons sugar
1 tablespoon lemon juice
1 tablespoon Grand Marnier
  Fresh mint

Sprinkle gelatin over white wine in small saucepan to soften. Add lemon juice and peel. Heat gently until gelatin is dissolved. Beat egg yolks with 3 tablespoons of the sugar until mixture forms a ribbon. Stir in gelatin mixture. Beat egg whites until foamy. Add remaining 5 tablespoons sugar; beat until mixture forms soft peaks. Fold egg yolk mixture into whipped cream. Fold in ½ of egg white mixture. Carefully fold in remaining egg white mixture. Refrigerate 2 hours.

SAUCE: Combine all sauce ingredients except mint in blender; puree. Strain through sieve to remove seeds. To serve, spoon sauce on individual serving plates. Place scoop of mousse on sauce. Garnish with fresh mint.

Cranberry Pecan Pie

8 Servings

Cafe Luxeford, Anne Buchanan

Cafe Luxeford is located downtown Minneapolis in the Hotel Luxeford

1 (9-inch) unbaked pie shell
1 cup fresh or frozen whole cranberries, thawed
3 eggs
⅔ cup packed brown sugar
⅛ teaspoon salt
1 cup light corn syrup
¼ cup butter or margarine, melted
1 cup pecan pieces
  Whipped cream

Prepare pie shell. Heat oven to 325°F. Place cranberries evenly in unbaked pie shell; set aside. Beat eggs in large bowl. Add brown sugar, salt, corn syrup and butter; mix well. Pour over cranberries. Sprinkle pecan pieces evenly over top. Bake in a slow oven, 325°F for 90 minutes or until knife inserted in center comes out clean. Serve with whipped cream.

Apple Almond Tart

6 to 8 Servings

Lucia's, Minneapolis, Lucia Watson

Lucia's is special. Her south Minneapolis dining room serves fresh and artful gourmet American food.

Pastry for 10-inch 1-crust pie
Apricot jam
4 egg yolks, beaten
½ cup sugar
½ cup chopped blanched almonds
⅓ cup raisins
Grated peel of ½ lemon
Juice of 1 lemon
2 large apples, peeled and shredded
½ teaspoon cinnamon
¼ cup butter or margarine, melted
Whipped cream or ice cream

Heat oven to 350°F. Press pastry into 10-inch fluted tart pan. Brush crust with jam. Combine remaining ingredients except whipped cream in large bowl; pour into unbaked crust. Bake at 350°F. for 30 minutes. Serve warm with whipped cream or ice cream.

Persimmon Pudding with Brandy Whipped Cream Sauce

8 to 12 Servings

Persimmons are usually available from November to January.

SAUCE

1 egg
1 cup sifted powdered sugar
Dash salt
⅓ cup butter or margarine, melted
1 tablespoon brandy
1 cup whipping cream

CAKE

½ cup butter, melted
1 cup sugar
1 cup all-purpose flour
¼ teaspoon salt
1 teaspoon cinnamon
¼ teaspoon nutmeg
2 teaspoons baking soda
2 teaspoons warm water
3 tablespoons brandy
1 cup persimmon pulp (3 to 4 very ripe persimmons)
1 teaspoon vanilla
2 eggs, slightly beaten

SAUCE: Beat egg until light and fluffy. Beat in powdered sugar, salt, butter and brandy. Whip cream until stiff; gently fold into egg mixture. Cover and refrigerate until serving time. Stir before spooning onto pudding.

CAKE: Grease 5 to 6-cup mold. Combine butter and sugar in large bowl. Combine flour, salt, cinnamon and nutmeg. Blend into butter-sugar mixture. Dissolve soda in water. Add with brandy and persimmon to sugar-flour mixture. Add vanilla and eggs to sugar-flour mixture; mix well. Pour batter into prepared mold. Cover with foil; place in large saucepan containing 2 to 3 inches boiling water. Cover pan; steam 2½ hours. Add additional boiling water if necessary. Unmold pudding; serve warm with sauce.

Arboretum Tea Room Orange and Walnut Cake

12 Servings

Arboretum Tea Room,
Chanhassen, Mary Mueller

A restaurant in a setting
featuring beautiful scenery
year round.

1¼ cups boiling water
1 cup quick-cooking rolled oats
½ cup butter, softened
1 cup sugar
½ cup packed brown sugar
2 eggs
¼ cup partially thawed frozen orange juice concentrate
1 teaspoon vanilla
1¾ cups all-purpose flour
1 teaspoon baking powder
1 teaspoon baking soda
½ teaspoon salt
½ teaspoon cinnamon
½ cup chopped walnuts

ORANGE WALNUT TOPPING

½ cup packed brown sugar
½ cup butter
¼ cup partially thawed frozen orange juice concentrate
1 cup flaked coconut
½ cup chopped walnuts
Half-and-half

Heat oven to 325 °F. Grease and flour 13 x 9-inch pan. Pour boiling water over oats; set aside. Cream butter with sugar and ½ cup brown sugar. Beat in eggs. Beat in orange juice concentrate and vanilla. Combine flour, baking powder, baking soda, salt and cinnamon; add to creamed mixture alternately with oats, beginning and ending with flour mixture. Fold in nuts. Pour batter into prepared pan. Bake at 325 °F. for 35 to 40 minutes or until toothpick inserted in center comes out clean. Cool completely.

TOPPING: Combine brown sugar, butter and orange juice concentrate in saucepan. Heat mixture to boiling; boil 1 minute. Stir in coconut, walnuts and enough half-and-half so topping spreads easily; spread over cooled cake.

Grand Marnier Fudge Sauce

About 4 Cups

12 oz. (12 squares) semi-sweet chocolate
2 oz. (2 squares) unsweetened chocolate
3 tablespoons strong coffee
2 cups whipping cream
2 tablespoons Grand Marnier

TIP: *Sauce keeps indefinitely, covered, in refrigerator.*

Melt chocolate in coffee in top of double boiler over hot water. Add cream and Grand Marnier; whisk until smooth.

Grasshopper Torte

8 Servings

The cool mint flavor of this torte is a great conclusion to a meal of hot spicy dishes.

CRUST

1 cup finely crushed chocolate wafer crumbs (about 16 wafers)
2 tablespoons butter or margarine, melted

FILLING

1¼ cups half-and-half
2½ cups firmly packed (about 36) large marshmallows
½ cup green creme de menthe
⅓ cup white creme de cacao
2 egg whites
3 tablespoons sugar
1½ cups whipping cream, whipped
Whipped cream
Shaved chocolate

CRUST: Combine crumbs and butter; press in bottom of 8 or 9-inch springform pan.
FILLING: Heat half-and-half and marshmallows in saucepan over medium-low heat, stirring constantly until marshmallows are melted. Place pan in cold water and stir until mixture is cool. Blend in creme de menthe and creme de cacao. Refrigerate until mixture begins to thicken. Beat egg whites until soft peaks form; gradually beat in sugar until stiff and glossy. Fold marshmallow mixture and egg whites into whipped cream. Pour into crust. Cover and freeze until firm, at least 8 hours. Remove from freezer 10 minutes before serving. Remove sides of pan. Cut into wedges; garnish with dollop of whipped cream and shaved chocolate.

Lemon Creme Dessert

6 Servings

1 cup milk
1 cup whipping cream
1 cup sugar
Grated peel and juice of 2 lemons
6 large lemons
Fresh mint leaves or candied violets
Lemon leaves, if desired

Combine milk, whipping cream and sugar until sugar is almost dissolved. Pour into freezer tray or metal bowl; freeze until mushy. Stir in lemon peel and juice. Beat well with rotary beater; freeze 2 hours. Remove from freezer and beat again. Return to freezer and freeze thoroughly. Slice top off 6 lemons and remove pulp with grapefruit knife. If necessary, cut a thin slice from bottoms so lemons will stand upright. Fill shells with frozen cream. Garnish each with a mint sprig or candied violet; place on lemon leaf on individual dessert plate.

Orange Alaska

6   medium oranges

FILLING

1   cup orange sherbet
1   cup orange yogurt
¼   cup fresh orange juice
¼   cup orange-flavored liqueur
1   teaspoon grated orange peel

MERINGUE

2   egg whites
¼   teaspoon cream of tartar
3   tablespoons sugar
¼   teaspoon vanilla

Cut tops off oranges; scoop out pulp. Reserve juice. If necessary cut a very thin slice from bottoms so oranges will stand upright.

FILLING: Combine sherbet, yogurt, juice, liqueur and orange peel. Pour mixture into orange shells; freeze.

MERINGUE: Beat egg whites until frothy. Add cream of tartar and beat until soft peaks form. Gradually add sugar and vanilla: beat until stiff and glossy. Completely cover filling with meringue, sealing to edge of shells. Freeze. To serve, place oven rack in lowest position; heat broiler. Place oranges on ungreased cookie sheet; broil until meringues are light brown, about 3 minutes.

Fresh Strawberries with Raspberry Puree and Pistachio Nuts

1   (12-oz.) pkg. frozen raspberries, thawed
1½ tablespoons sugar
1   tablespoon orange juice
1½ tablespoons lemon juice
3   pints fresh strawberries, halved
2   tablespoons powdered sugar
3   tablespoons Grand Marnier
2   teaspoons unsalted, slivered pistachio nuts

Drain raspberries; puree in blender. Stir in sugar, orange and lemon juices; refrigerate. Place strawberries in bowl; sift powdered sugar over each layer. Add Grand Marnier; refrigerate. To serve, pour raspberry puree over strawberries; sprinkle with nuts.

Harvest Cheesecake

12 Servings

CRUST

1½ cups graham cracker crumbs
½ cup finely chopped pecans
3 tablespoons sugar
¼ teaspoon pumpkin pie spice
6 tablespoons butter or margarine, melted

FILLING

1 (16-oz.) carton creamed cottage cheese
4 eggs
3 (8-oz.) pkg. cream cheese, softened
1 cup sugar
2 tablespoons flour
1 teaspoon grated orange peel
1½ teaspoons pumpkin pie spice
¼ teaspoon salt
1 (16-oz.) can pumpkin

TOPPING

2 cups dairy sour cream
¼ cup orange marmalade
1 medium orange

CRUST: Heat oven to 300°F. Combine crumbs, pecans, 3 tablespoons sugar and ¼ teaspoon pumpkin pie spice; stir in butter. Press mixture evenly in bottom and 1½ inches up side of 10-inch springform pan. Bake at 300°F. for 10 minutes. Cool.

FILLING: Combine cottage cheese and eggs in blender at high speed, or food processor, until smooth. Beat cream cheese, 1 cup sugar, flour, orange peel, 1½ teaspoons pumpkin pie spice, salt and cottage cheese mixture in large bowl until smooth. Fold in pumpkin. Pour into prepared crust. Bake at 300°F. for 1½ hours. Turn oven off. Cool cheesecake in oven 1 hour, keeping oven door slightly ajar. Remove cheesecake from oven. Heat oven to 350°F.

TOPPING: Combine sour cream and orange marmalade; spread over cheesecake. Bake at 350°F. for 10 minutes. Cool slightly; refrigerate. To serve, remove sides of springform pan. Slice orange into thin rings; remove pulp. Decorate cake with peel cut into semicircles.

Praline Pumpkin Pie

6 to 8 Servings

1   (9-inch) unbaked pie shell

PRALINE LAYER

⅔   cup finely chopped pecans
⅔   cup packed brown sugar
¼   cup butter or margarine, softened

FILLING

2   eggs
1   cup canned pumpkin
⅔   cup packed brown sugar
1   teaspoon flour
½   teaspoon salt
½   teaspoon cinnamon
¼   teaspoon ground cloves
1   cup half-and-half

    Whipped cream

Prepare pie shell. Heat oven to 400°F.
    PRALINE LAYER: Combine all praline layer ingredients; press into unbaked pie shell.
    FILLING: Beat eggs in large bowl until frothy. Add remaining filling ingredients; beat only until well mixed. Pour over praline layer. Bake at 400°F. for 50 to 55 minutes or until knife inserted in center comes out clean. Cool. Serve with whipped cream.

Pumpkin Cream Torte

15 to 18 Servings

This is sweet and rich. A wonderful Thanksgiving dessert for those who don't like pumpkin pie.

CRUST

24 (2 x 2-inch) graham crackers, crushed
½   cup butter or margarine, melted
½   cup sugar

CREAM CHEESE FILLING

1   (8-oz.) pkg. cream cheese, softened
¾   cup sugar
2   eggs, beaten

PUMPKIN FILLING

1   (16-oz.) can pumpkin
½   cup sugar
1   tablespoon cinnamon
½   teaspoon salt
3   eggs, separated
½   cup milk
1   envelope unflavored gelatin
¼   cup cold water
¼   cup sugar
1   cup whipping cream, whipped

CRUST: Heat oven to 350°F. Combine crumbs, butter and ½ cup sugar; press in bottom of 13 x 9-inch pan.
  CREAM CHEESE FILLING: Combine all filling ingredients; mix well. Pour over crust. Bake at 350°F. for 20 minutes. Cool.
  PUMPKIN FILLING: Combine pumpkin, ½ cup sugar, cinnamon, salt, egg yolks and milk in saucepan; cook and stir over medium heat until mixture thickens. Soften gelatin in water. Remove pumpkin mixture from heat; stir in gelatin, mixing well. Cool. Beat egg whites until soft peaks form. Gradually add ¼ cup sugar; beat until stiff. Fold into cooled pumpkin mixture. Pour over baked cream cheese mixture. Refrigerate until firm. To serve, top with whipped cream.

TIP: *Torte can be prepared 1 day before serving. Cover and refrigerate.*

Brandied Apricot Sauce

3 Cups

Muffulleta In the Park, St. Paul, Roberta Grewing

Muffulleta is a wonderful place for Sunday brunch.

1   (16-oz.) jar apricot preserves
6   tablespoons butter or margarine
¼   cup raisins
1   cup brandy

Heat preserves and butter in medium saucepan over low heat until butter is melted, stirring constantly. Stir in raisins and brandy. Store in covered container in refrigerator up to 3 weeks. Serve warm over ice cream or cheesecake.

Marlys' Pumpkin Cookies

3 to 4 Dozen
Lund's, Minneapolis, Pat Lund

Lund's, one of Minneapolis'
favorite supermarkets.

1   cup shortening
½   cup packed brown sugar
½   cup sugar
1   egg
1   cup canned pumpkin
1   teaspoon vanilla
2   cups flour
1   teaspoon baking soda
1   teaspoon salt
½   cup chopped nuts
½   cup chopped dates or raisins

FROSTING

½   cup packed brown sugar
1   tablespoon butter
¼   cup milk
     Powdered sugar

Heat oven to 375°F. Lightly grease cookie sheets. Combine shortening, sugars, egg, pumpkin and vanilla in large bowl. Combine flour, soda and salt; blend into pumpkin mixture. Stir in nuts and dates. Drop by teaspoonfuls onto prepared cookie sheets. Bake at 375°F. for 12 to 15 minutes. Cool.

FROSTING: Combine brown sugar, butter and milk in medium saucepan; heat to boiling. Cool. Blend in enough powdered sugar to make spreading consistency. Frost cooled cookies.

Monster Cookies

6 to 8 Dozen

Rudy Boschwitz, U.S. Senator
from Minnesota, gave us these
favorites.

2⅔   cups crunchy peanut butter
1   cup butter or margarine, softened
2¼   cups packed brown sugar
2   cups sugar
6   eggs, beaten
1½   teaspoons corn syrup
1½   teaspoons vanilla
8   to 10 cups rolled oats
4   teaspoons baking soda
1   (8-oz.) pkg. M & M candies
1   (6-oz.) pkg. (1 cup) semi-sweet chocolate chips

Heat oven to 350°F. Combine peanut butter, butter, brown sugar and sugar in very large bowl. Stir in eggs, corn syrup and vanilla. Combine oats and soda in separate bowl; stir into butter mixture. Stir in candy and chocolate chips. Drop by heaping tablespoonfuls onto ungreased cookie sheets. Bake at 350°F. for 8 to 10 minutes or until just brown. Do not overbake.

Turtle Bars

3 Dozen

2 cups all-purpose flour
1 cup packed brown sugar
½ cup butter or margarine, softened
1 cup pecan halves
⅔ cup butter or margarine
½ cup packed brown sugar
1 (12-oz.) pkg. (2 cups) semi-sweet chocolate chips

Heat oven to 350 °F. Combine flour, 1 cup brown sugar and ½ cup butter; mix at medium speed 2 to 3 minutes. Pat firmly into ungreased 13 x 9-inch pan. Sprinkle evenly with pecans. Combine ⅔ cup butter and ½ cup brown sugar in saucepan; cook over medium heat, stirring constantly until mixture begins to boil. Boil 1 minute, stirring constantly. Pour syrup over pecans and crust. Bake at 350 °F. for 20 to 25 minutes until caramel is bubbly and crust is golden. Remove from oven and sprinkle with chocolate chips. Allow chips to melt slightly, 2 to 3 minutes; swirl chips slightly into bars as they melt. Cool completely. Cut into small squares.

Lucky Lemon Surprise

12 Servings

2 (3-oz.) pkg. ladyfingers
2 (14-oz.) cans sweetened condensed milk
8 eggs, separated
2 teaspoons grated lemon peel
¾ cup plus 3 tablespoons fresh lemon juice
¼ teaspoon cream of tartar
Powdered sugar
Thin lemon slice

Heat oven to 375 °F. Grease 9-inch springform pan; cover bottom of pan with ladyfingers. Stand remaining ladyfingers around sides of pan, cutting bottom ends so tops of ladyfingers are even with top of pan. Combine condensed milk, egg yolks, lemon peel and juice in large bowl. Combine egg whites and cream of tartar in medium bowl; beat until stiff. Fold in lemon mixture. Pour batter into prepared pan. Bake at 375 °F. for 25 minutes or until top is lightly browned. Cool completely; cover with foil and freeze. (Will keep frozen up to 3 months.) To serve, remove side of springform pan. Sprinkle top of dessert with powdered sugar. Garnish with twisted lemon slice in center. Any remaining dessert can be covered and refrozen.

Butter Crunch Toffee

24 Pieces

Make a double recipe as this candy goes fast!

1   cup butter
1⅓ cups sugar
3   tablespoons water
1   tablespoon light corn syrup
1   (6-oz.) pkg. (1 cup) semi-sweet chocolate chips
½   cup sliced almonds, toasted

Heating pan will allow toffee to spread easily in pan.

Grease 15 x 10-inch jelly roll pan. Melt butter in medium saucepan. Stir in sugar, water and corn syrup; cook over medium heat stirring occasionally until mixture reaches 300°F. (hard crack stage), about 20 minutes. Pour immediately into prepared pan. Sprinkle chocolate chips over mixture and let stand 1 to 2 minutes; spread to frost. Sprinkle with toasted almonds. Refrigerate until cooled. Break into pieces.

Creme de Menthe Bars

5 Dozen

A no-bake bar!

2   cups graham cracker crumbs
1½ cups chopped walnuts
1   cup coconut
½   cup powdered sugar
¼   cup unsweetened cocoa powder
¾   cup butter or margarine, melted
1   teaspoon vanilla
1   egg, well beaten
2   cups powdered sugar
2   teaspoons dry vanilla pudding mix (not instant)
½   cup butter or margarine, softened
3   tablespoons creme de menthe
1   (12-oz.) pkg. (2 cups) semi-sweet chocolate chips
½   cup butter or margarine

Combine crumbs, nuts, coconut, ½ cup powdered sugar, cocoa, ¾ cup butter, vanilla and egg in large bowl; mix well. Pat into ungreased 13 x 9-inch pan. Refrigerate 1 to 2 hours. Beat together 2 cups powdered sugar, pudding mix, ½ cup butter and creme de menthe; pour over crust. Refrigerate 2 hours. Heat chocolate chips and ½ cup butter together in small saucepan over low heat; stir until smooth. Spread over creme de menthe layer. Refrigerate until set. Cut into small squares.

Interlachen's Pecan Torte

8 to 10 Servings

*Interlachen Country Club,
Edina, Sally Nordquist*

6 eggs, separated
1 cup sugar
  Dash salt
½ cup broken pecans
½ cup crumbled soda crackers
½ teaspoon vanilla, or to taste
1 cup whipping cream
2 tablespoons sugar

CARAMEL SAUCE

2 cups packed brown sugar
2 cups whipping cream
½ cup butter

Heat oven to 375 °F. Grease and flour edges and bottom of 2 (8-inch) square pans and line with parchment paper. Beat egg yolks with 1 cup sugar and salt until thick. Beat egg whites until stiff; fold into egg yolk mixture with pecans, crackers and vanilla. Pour into prepared pans. Bake at 375 °F. for 30 minutes. Cool completely. Remove layers from pans. Whip 1 cup cream with 2 tablespoons sugar; spread half of whipped cream over 1 layer. Top with second layer; spread with remaining whipped cream.

SAUCE: Combine brown sugar with 2 cups whipping cream and butter. Cook over medium heat, stirring to dissolve sugar, about 5 minutes. Cool. Cut torte into 8 to 10 pieces. Serve topped with sauce.

Mixed Nut Bars

2 Dozen

1½ cups all-purpose flour
¾ cup sugar
½ teaspoon salt
½ cup butter or margarine
1 (6-oz.) pkg. (1 cup) butterscotch chips
½ cup light corn syrup
2 tablespoons butter or margarine
1 teaspoon water
1 (12-oz.) can mixed nuts

Heat oven to 350 °F. Grease 13 x 9-inch pan. Combine flour, sugar and salt; cut in ½ cup butter. Press into prepared pan. Bake at 350 °F. for 10 minutes. Combine butterscotch chips, corn syrup, 2 tablespoons butter and water in medium saucepan; heat and stir over medium heat until mixture is smooth. Spread mixture over crust and top with nuts. Bake at 350 °F. for 10 minutes or until bars are bubbling. Cool slightly; cut into bars. Cool completely.

Christmas Pecan Cake

12 to 16 Servings

A very special Holiday cake — Slice and serve as part of a buffet.

2 cups butter or margarine, softened
2½ cups light brown sugar
6 egg yolks, well beaten
4 cups all-purpose flour
3 tablespoons lemon extract
6 egg whites, stiffly beaten
3 to 4 cups chopped pecans
8 oz. candied cherries, chopped
8 oz. candied pineapple, chopped
Cheese cloth
Rum

TIP: *Cake can be stored in refrigerator up to 1 week.*

Heat oven to 250°F. Butter 10-inch tube pan. Cream butter and brown sugar in large bowl. Beat in egg yolks. Beat in flour and extract. Fold in small amount of egg whites. Fold in remaining egg whites; carefully fold in nuts and fruit. Bake at 250°F. for 2 to 3 hours or until toothpick inserted in center comes out clean. Cool completely before removing from pan. Soak cheese cloth in rum; wrap around cooled cake. Wrap cake in foil. Store in refrigerator.

Merry Cheesecake Bars

3 Dozen

1 cup all-purpose flour
½ cup packed brown sugar
⅓ cup butter, softened
½ cup chopped pecans

FILLING

1 (8-oz.) pkg. cream cheese, softened
¼ cup sugar
2 tablespoons milk
2 tablespoons lemon juice
½ teaspoon vanilla
1 egg

Heat oven to 350°F. Combine flour, brown sugar and butter; blend at low speed until particles are fine. Stir in nuts. Reserve 1 cup mixture for topping. Press remaining mixture into ungreased 8-inch square pan. Bake at 350°F. for 8 to 10 minutes or until light brown.

FILLING: Combine all filling ingredients; blend until smooth. Spread filling over partially baked crust. Sprinkle with reserved crumb mixture. Bake at 350°F. for 24 to 30 minutes or until light brown. Cool. Cut into bars. Store in refrigerator.

Chocolate Yogurt Cheesecake with Chocolate Glaze

10 to 12 Servings

A long-stemmed red rose is a spectacular garnish on this cake.

CRUST

1 cup chocolate wafer crumbs, 16 (2¼-inch) wafers
¼ cup butter or margarine, melted

FILLING

2 (8-oz.) pkg. cream cheese, softened
1 cup sugar
3 eggs, at room temperature
1½ teaspoons vanilla
6 oz. (6 squares) semi-sweet chocolate, melted
1 cup plain yogurt

GLAZE

3 oz. (3 squares) semi-sweet chocolate
2 tablespoons butter or margarine
1 tablespoon corn syrup
½ teaspoon vanilla

  Whole fresh strawberries
  Whipped cream

CRUST: Heat oven to 300°F. Grease 8-inch springform pan. Blend crumbs and butter; press firmly in bottom of prepared springform pan. Refrigerate.

FILLING: Beat cream cheese and sugar in large bowl until smooth. Add eggs and vanilla; continue beating. Stir in 6 oz. chocolate and yogurt until well blended. Pour into prepared crust and place on middle oven rack. Place pan of water on bottom oven rack. Bake at 300°F. for 50 to 60 minutes or until cheesecake pulls away from sides of pan. Do not open oven during baking. Turn oven off; cool cheesecake in oven with door ajar. Run a knife around sides of pan; carefully remove sides and place cheesecake on serving plate.

GLAZE: Combine all glaze ingredients in small saucepan over low heat, stirring constantly until mixture is melted and smooth. Remove from heat; cool slightly. Spread glaze over cooled cheesecake, using back of spoon to create a pattern. Refrigerate several hours or overnight. Garnish with strawberries and whipped cream.

Mocha Cheesecake

10 to 12 Servings

*Everybody's favorite —
chocolate-coffee cheesecake
— rich and creamy*

CRUST

1¼ cups zwieback crumbs
1 tablespoon sugar
¼ cup butter or margarine, melted

FILLING

12 oz. (12 squares) semi-sweet chocolate
½ cup hot coffee
2 (8-oz.) pkg. cream cheese, softened
1 cup sugar
4 eggs
2 teaspoons vanilla
¼ teaspoon salt

1 cup whipping cream, whipped
Shaved chocolate

TIP: *Best served at room
temperature; refrigerate for
longer storage.*

CRUST: Heat oven to 325 °F. Grease bottom and sides of 10-inch
springform pan. Combine crumbs and 1 tablespoon sugar. Sprinkle some of
crumbs around pan to coat sides. Add melted butter to remaining crumbs;
blend well. Press mixture in bottom of prepared pan.
FILLING: Melt chocolate in coffee in top of double boiler over hot
water. Beat cream cheese until light and fluffy. Gradually add 1 cup sugar,
beating constantly. Scrape sides of bowl and continue beating. Add eggs to
mixture one at a time, beating well after each. Stir in vanilla and salt. Beat
in melted chocolate until blended. Pour mixture into prepared crust. Bake
at 325 °F. for 55 minutes. Turn oven off; let cheesecake cool in oven with
door ajar 2 to 3 hours. Remove sides of pan. Spread top with whipped
cream; sprinkle with shaved chocolate.

Vanilla Sauce for Strawberries

*12 Servings
(About 2½ cups sauce.)*

*A wonderful sauce for any
seasonal fresh fruit!*

¾ cup sugar
1½ teaspoons unflavored gelatin
½ cup water
1 cup whipping cream
½ cup dairy sour cream
1 teaspoon vanilla

Combine sugar, gelatin and water in small saucepan. Heat to boiling, stirring constantly. Remove from heat; stir in whipping cream. Set aside to cool.
Combine sour cream and vanilla in small bowl; whisk into cooled cream
mixture until thoroughly combined. Serve at room temperature over fresh
strawberries. Refrigerate leftovers. If sauce gels, whisk vigorously until
smooth.

Chocolate Chip Cheesecake

10 to 12 Servings

1½ cups finely crushed cream-filled chocolate sandwich cookies (about 18 cookies)
¼ cup butter or margarine, melted
3 (8-oz.) pkg. cream cheese, softened
1 (14-oz.) can sweetened condensed milk
3 eggs
1 (12-oz.) pkg. (2 cups) mini chocolate chips

Heat oven to 300°F. Grease 9-inch springform pan. Combine crumbs and butter; press in bottom of prepared pan. Beat cream cheese in large bowl until fluffy. Beat in condensed milk until smooth. Beat in eggs, one at a time, mixing well after each. Stir in 1½ cups chocolate chips. Pour mixture into prepared crust. Sprinkle remaining chocolate chips over top. Bake at 300°F. for 1 hour. Cool completely. Remove sides of pan.

TIP: *Cheesecake can be prepared several days ahead. Refrigerate, covered.*

Walnut Torte

10 to 12 Servings

¾ cup sugar
7 eggs, separated
6 oz. walnuts, finely ground
3 tablespoons dry bread crumbs

FROSTING

½ cup unsalted butter, softened
4 oz. (4 squares) semi-sweet chocolate, melted
½ cup powdered sugar
1 tablespoon instant coffee granules or powder
2 eggs
Walnuts

Heat oven to 350°F. Grease 2 (9-inch) round cake pans with removable bottoms. Beat sugar and egg yolks until light colored, about 5 minutes. Fold in walnuts. In separate bowl, beat egg whites until stiff but not dry, fold into yolk mixture. Fold in crumbs. Pour mixture into prepared pans. Bake at 350°F. for 20 to 25 minutes. Cool completely; remove from pans.

FROSTING: Combine all frosting ingredients except walnuts; beat with mixer until well blended and of spreading consistency. Place one cake layer on serving plate. Spread with ½ of frosting. Place second layer over frosting. Spread remaining frosting over top; garnish with walnuts.

TIP: *Nine-inch round cake pans, greased and lined with parchment or waxed paper can be used in place of cake pans with removable bottoms.*

Macadamia Fudge Cake

12 Servings

Worth every calorie!

1 cup all-purpose flour
¾ cup sugar
¼ cup unsweetened cocoa powder
1½ teaspoons instant coffee powder or granules
½ teaspoon baking powder
½ teaspoon baking soda
¼ teaspoon salt
¾ cup dairy sour cream
½ cup butter or margarine, softened
½ teaspoon vanilla
1 egg

TOPPING

½ cup sugar
4 oz. (4 squares) semi-sweet chocolate
1 cup whipping cream
2 tablespoons butter or margarine
1 tablespoon corn syrup
1 teaspoon vanilla
1 (7-oz.) jar macadamia nuts, halved

Heat oven to 350°F. Grease 9-inch round cake pan; line bottom of pan with waxed paper and grease paper. Combine all cake ingredients in large bowl; mix at low speed until well blended. Pour batter into prepared pan. Bake at 350°F. 30 to 35 minutes or until toothpick inserted in center comes out clean. Cool cake 10 minutes on wire rack. Remove cake from pan; cool completely on rack.

TOPPING: Combine sugar, chocolate, cream, butter and corn syrup in medium saucepan over medium heat; stirring constantly until mixture boils. Continue stirring and reduce heat; cook 5 minutes. Remove saucepan from heat; stir in vanilla. Cool mixture 10 minutes; stir in nuts. Place cooled cake on serving plate. Pour topping evenly over cake. Refrigerate until topping is firm.

Brandy Shake

16 (10-oz.) Servings

Fitzgerald's Restaurant, St. Paul, Tom Robertson

A decidedly adult shake; serve as a dessert.

Fitzgerald's is located in Galtier Plaza in downtown St. Paul.

4½ quarts Häagen Dazs vanilla ice cream
1 cup brandy
½ cup Kahlua
½ cup dark creme de cacao

Soften ice cream at room temperature until it can be easily scooped. (Do not allow to melt completely.) Beat ice cream with mixer until smooth and creamy. Blend in liqueurs until thoroughly combined. Transfer to 2-quart container with tight fitting lid. Freeze. Serve in 10-oz. pilsner-type glasses.

Very Intense Brownies

3 to 4 Dozen

Al Sicherman is a writer for the Minneapolis Star Tribune who combines food knowledge and humor.

"The topping color lightens as it is beaten but don't let it fool you. This stuff is still more deeply chocolate than the average soul has any right to expect!"

BROWNIES

1	(12-oz.) pkg. (2 cups) semi-sweet chocolate chips
⅔	cup butter
1	cup sugar
4	eggs
2	teaspoons vanilla
1	cup all-purpose flour
1	teaspoon baking powder
½	teaspoon salt
1	cup chopped pecans
1	(12-oz.) pkg. (2 cups) semi-sweet chocolate chips

GLOPPY TOPPING

1½	cups whipping cream
¼	cup unsalted butter
1	(12-oz.) pkg. (2 cups) semi-sweet chocolate chips

BROWNIES: Heat oven to 350°F. Grease 13 x 9-inch pan. Melt 1 pkg. chocolate chips with ⅔ cup butter in saucepan over low heat, stirring until blended. Remove from heat; pour into large bowl. Beat in sugar with mixer. Beat in eggs, 2 at a time, until well mixed. Stir in vanilla. Combine flour, baking powder and salt; blend into chocolate mixture until well mixed. Stir in nuts and 1 pkg. chocolate chips. Spread batter evenly in prepared pan. Bake at 350°F. for about 35 minutes or until toothpick inserted in center of bars (not in a chocolate chip) comes out clean. Cool.

GLOPPY TOPPING: Combine cream and unsalted butter in medium saucepan; heat to boiling over medium heat. Remove from heat; stir in 1 pkg. chocolate chips until completely melted. Pour into small bowl; beat briefly with electric mixer. Refrigerate to chill, stirring occasionally until mixture is consistency of *very* thick cream, 45 to 60 minutes. (If mixture gets too hard, warm it a few minutes.) Whip with electic mixer, until stiff. Spread, spoon or pipe in individual swirls on brownies.

Brownie Torte

8 to 10 Servings

1 cup all-purpose flour
¼ cup packed light brown sugar
¼ cup butter or margarine, softened
1 oz. (1 square) unsweetened chocolate, grated
¾ cup finely chopped pecans
2 tablespoons milk
1 teaspoon vanilla

FILLING

3 oz. (3 squares) unsweetened chocolate
½ cup butter or margarine, softened
1½ cups sugar
3 eggs
2 teaspoons vanilla
¾ cup all-purpose flour
1 teaspoon baking powder
¼ teaspoon salt

GLAZE

4 oz. (4 squares) semi-sweet chocolate
Dash salt
¼ cup butter or margarine, softened
2 tablespoons vegetable oil
Pecan halves

Heat oven to 350 °F. Grease 9-inch springform pan. Combine flour, brown sugar, ¼ cup butter and 1 oz. chocolate in large bowl until mixture resembles coarse crumbs. Add pecans, milk and 1 teaspoon vanilla; mix well. (Dough should be soft but not sticky.) Add additional milk if dough appears dry. Press in bottom and up sides of prepared pan.

FILLING: Melt 3 oz. chocolate; cool slightly. Beat ½ cup butter and sugar in large bowl until pale and fluffy; beat in eggs. Beat in melted chocolate and 2 teaspoons vanilla until smooth. Combine flour, baking powder and salt; beat into chocolate mixture. Pour mixture into prepared crust. Bake at 350 °F. for 25 minutes. (Center will not be set when done.)

GLAZE: Melt 4 oz. chocolate; cool slightly. Beat in salt, ¼ cup butter and oil until smooth. Spread glaze over hot torte. Cool 15 minutes before removing sides of pan. Cool completely. Garnish with pecan halves.

Chocolate Souffle with Creme de Cacao

12 to 14 Servings

This souffle is also a great frozen dessert.

2   envelopes unflavored gelatin
½   cup water
⅔   cup creme de cacao
½   cup packed dark brown sugar
1   (12-oz.) pkg. (2 cups) semi-sweet chocolate chips
8   eggs, separated
½   teaspoon salt
¾   cup packed dark brown sugar
2   cups whipping cream, whipped
½   cup chopped pistachio nuts or toasted slivered almonds

Wrap and secure with tape a 3-inch collar of foil around top of 2-quart souffle dish, allowing collar to stand 2 inches above dish.

Combine gelatin, water, creme de cacao and ½ cup brown sugar in saucepan. Cook over low heat, stirring constantly until gelatin and sugar dissolve. Stir in chocolate chips until melted; remove from heat. Beat in egg yolks, one at a time. Add salt to egg whites and beat until stiff but not dry. Gradually beat in ¾ cup brown sugar; continue beating until very stiff. Fold egg whites into gelatin mixture. Fold in whipped cream. Pour into prepared souffle dish or serving bowl. Refrigerate several hours or overnight. Sprinkle with pistachios. Serve with additional whipped cream, if desired.

The Chocolate Roll

10 Servings

Gallery 8, Walker Art Center, Minneapolis

Gallery 8 is located at the Walker Art Center which is famous for its contemporary art collection.

6   eggs, separated
6   tablespoons sugar
6   tablespoons unsweetened cocoa powder
2   tablespoons cornstarch
1   teaspoon vanilla

FILLING

½   cup powdered sugar
⅓   cup unsweetened cocoa powder
1½ cups whipping cream
1   teaspoon vanilla

Heat oven to 350°F. Line 15 x 10-inch jelly roll pan with parchment. Beat egg yolks thoroughly. Combine sugar, cocoa and cornstarch; gradually blend into egg yolks. Stir in vanilla. Beat egg whites until stiff; stir a small amount into yolk mixture. Fold egg yolk mixture into egg whites. Pour batter into prepared pan. Bake at 350°F. for 10 minutes. Turn out immediately onto damp towel; peel off parchment. Roll up hot cake, starting at wide edge. Place on wire rack; cool completely.

FILLING: Combine all filling ingredients in bowl; refrigerate. Whip until stiff. Unroll cake; remove towel. Spread filling evenly over cake. Roll cake up again. Place seam side down on serving plate. Cover and refrigerate until serving time.

TIPS: Coarsely chopped walnuts can be folded into whipped cream. Roll can be frosted with whipped cream or sprinkled with sifted cocoa.

Serve on white doilies.

Daquoise with Mocha Butter Cream

10 to 12 Servings

<u>MERINGUES</u>

6 egg whites
⅛ teaspoon salt
¼ teaspoon cream of tartar
3 tablespoons sugar
1 teaspoon vanilla
6 oz. finely ground almonds
1 cup superfine sugar
1½ tablespoons cornstarch

<u>BUTTER CREAM FILLING</u>

⅔ cup sugar
⅓ cup water
5 egg yolks
2 teaspoons instant coffee granules or powder
1 cup unsalted butter, softened
1 teaspoon vanilla
1 teaspoon Grand Marnier or brandy
  Powdered sugar or whipped cream
  Fresh strawberries and/or raspberries

<u>MERINGUES:</u> Heat oven to 350°F. Grease and flour 2 cookie sheets. Beat egg whites until foamy. Add salt and cream of tartar; continue beating until soft peaks form. Gradually add 3 tablespoons sugar, beating until stiff peaks form. Beat in 1 teaspoon vanilla. Combine almonds, superfine sugar and cornstarch; gradually fold into beaten egg whites. Spoon or pipe mixture onto prepared cookie sheets to form two 9-inch circles. Bake at 350°F. for 35 minutes. Cool 5 minutes on cookie sheets; carefully remove to racks to cool completely.

  <u>FILLING:</u> Combine ⅔ cup sugar and water in small saucepan; heat to boiling over high heat, stirring constantly until sugar dissolves. Continue to boil gently until mixture reaches 234°F. (soft ball stage). With mixer, beat egg yolks until very light, about 5 minutes. Gradually add hot syrup to yolks while beating. Continue beating until mixture begins to thicken. Add coffee; continue beating until mixture has cooled to room temperature. Add butter, 1 tablespoon at a time, while beating. Beat in vanilla and Grand Marnier.

  To assemble: Place one meringue on serving plate; spread with filling. Top with remaining meringue; refrigerate. Before serving, sprinkle with powdered sugar or top with dollop of whipped cream; garnish with fresh berries.

TIP: *Best if served within 24 hours.*

Frozen Chocolate Crepes with Butter Rum Sauce

16 to 18 Servings

This impressive dessert can be completely made in advance. The sauce is especially good.

CREPES

1	cup all-purpose flour
¼	cup sugar
2	tablespoons unsweetened cocoa powder
1	cup milk
1	tablespoon butter or margarine, melted
1	teaspoon vanilla
2	eggs

CHOCOLATE MOUSSE FILLING

1	(12-oz.) pkg. (2 cups) semi-sweet chocolate chips
½	teaspoon salt
1½	teaspoons vanilla
1½	cups whipping cream, heated to boiling
6	egg yolks
6	egg whites, beaten until stiff

BUTTER RUM SAUCE

1	cup packed brown sugar
¼	teaspoon salt
1	cup half-and-half
1	cup light corn syrup
¼	cup butter
3	tablespoons light rum
	Whipped cream
	Shaved chocolate

CREPES: Combine all crepe ingredients in blender; blend on low speed 30 seconds. Allow batter to stand at room temperature 1 hour before cooking crepes. Heat crepe pan or 7 or 8-inch skillet over medium-high heat. Grease pan lightly. Pour about 3 tablespoons batter into pan, tilting pan to spread evenly. When crepe is light brown and set, turn to brown other side. Remove from pan and cool on rack. Cover and refrigerate until ready to fill.

FILLING: Place chocolate chips, salt and vanilla in blender; blend on low speed 30 seconds. Add boiling cream; blend 30 seconds. Add egg yolks all at once; blend 5 seconds. Add a small amount of chocolate mixture to beaten egg whites. Carefully fold in remaining chocolate mixture. Refrigerate 2 to 3 hours or until set. To assemble crepes, place 1 heaping tablespoon filling on center of each crepe. Fold sides over. Place on waxed paper-lined cookie sheet or tray; cover tightly. Freeze until ready to serve.

SAUCE: Combine all sauce ingredients in medium saucepan. Cook over low heat, stirring occasionally, 5 minutes. Refrigerate until ready to serve. Heat sauce until warm; spoon 2 to 3 tablespoons onto individual serving plates. Place 1 crepe in sauce. Garnish with whipped cream and shaved chocolate.

Peanut Fudge Ice Cream Bars

12 to 16 Servings

1 (12-oz.) pkg. chocolate creme-filled sandwich cookies (9 oz. package of chocolate wafers can be substituted)
½ to ¾ cup butter or margarine, melted
½ gallon vanilla ice cream, softened
1½ cups salted Spanish peanuts

SAUCE

2 cups powdered sugar
⅔ cup chocolate chips
1 (12-oz.) can (1½ cups) evaporated milk
½ cup butter or margarine
1 teaspoon vanilla

Remove creme filling from cookies. Crush cookies into crumbs; toss with butter. Press into 13 x 9-inch pan. Freeze. When crust is frozen, spread with ice cream and top with peanuts. Return to freezer.

SAUCE: Combine all sauce ingredients except vanilla in 2-quart saucepan; heat to boiling. Boil mixture gently 8 minutes, stirring constantly. Remove from heat; cool slightly and stir in vanilla. When sauce is completely cool, pour over ice cream; freeze until firm. Cut into squares to serve.

White Chocolate-Raspberry Tart

10 Servings

Pastry for 9-inch 1-crust pie
1 (10-oz.) pkg. frozen raspberries, thawed
2 tablespoons cornstarch
1 cup fresh raspberries, if desired
½ cup butter or margarine, softened
⅓ cup sugar
4 oz. white chocolate, melted
2 eggs
2 oz. (2 squares) semi-sweet chocolate, cut up
2 tablespoons butter or margarine

Heat oven to 450°F. Roll out pastry; press in bottom and 1 inch up sides of 10-inch tart pan with removable bottom. Trim edges; prick crust with fork. Bake at 450°F. for 9 to 11 minutes or until lightly browned. Cool. Purée raspberries in blender; strain to remove seeds. Heat raspberry purée and cornstarch in saucepan, stirring until thickened. Cool. Spread in cooled crust. Place fresh raspberries in crust. Beat ½ cup butter and ⅓ cup sugar in small bowl until fluffy. Gradually add melted white chocolate until incorporated. Add eggs 1 at a time, beating at highest speed for 3 minutes after each addition. Pour over raspberries. Refrigerate until set. Combine semi-sweet chocolate and 2 tablespoons butter in 2-cup glass measuring cup. Microwave on MEDIUM 30 to 40 seconds or melt over boiling water. Stir until smooth. Carefully pour and spread over white chocolate layer. Leave a rim of white chocolate layer around edge. Refrigerate at least 2 hours. To serve, let stand at room temperature about 30 minutes before cutting.

Chocolate Fudge Pie

16 Servings (8/Pie)

2 (8-inch) unbaked pie shells
2½ oz. (2½ squares) unsweetened chocolate
1 cup butter or margarine
4 eggs
2 cups sugar
½ cup all-purpose flour
Dash salt
1 teaspoon vanilla
Vanilla ice cream

TIP: *Do not overbake, center of pie should be consistency of fudge.*

Prepare pie shells. Heat oven to 350°F. Melt chocolate and butter in saucepan over low heat, stirring occasionally. Remove from heat; cool to room temperature. Beat eggs slightly in large bowl with electric mixer. Blend in sugar, flour, salt and vanilla until well mixed. Stir in chocolate mixture until well blended. Divide mixture between pie shells. Bake at 350°F. for 30 minutes. Cool. Serve with ice cream.

Raspberry Cream Torte

9 Servings

¼ cup butter or margarine, melted
½ cup all-purpose flour
¼ cup packed brown sugar
⅓ cup chopped pecans
25 large marshmallows
1 (10-oz.) pkg. frozen raspberries, thawed and drained (reserve syrup)
1 cup whipping cream, whipped
   Whipping cream
   Fresh raspberries

Heat oven to 350°F. Combine butter, flour, brown sugar and pecans; mix well. Spread on cookie sheet. Bake at 350°F. for 15 minutes or until lightly browned (watch closely). Remove from cookie sheet; stir to crumble. Reserve 2 tablespoons crumb mixture. Place remaining mixture in 8-inch square pan; press lightly. Heat marshmallows and reserved raspberry syrup in large saucepan over medium heat until marshmallows are melted, stirring occasionally. Stir in raspberries; cool. Fold in 1 cup whipped cream. Pour over crumb mixture; refrigerate 4 to 6 hours, until firm, or freeze. To serve, cut into squares; garnish with whipped cream, fresh raspberries and reserved crumbs. If frozen, thaw slightly.

TIP: *Recipe can be doubled and prepared in 13 x 9-inch pan.*

Chocolate Angel Strata Pie

8 Servings

1 (10-inch) baked pie crust
2 egg whites
½ cup sugar
¼ teaspoon salt
¼ teaspoon cinnamon
½ teaspoon vinegar
1 (6-oz.) pkg. (1 cup) semi-sweet chocolate chips
2 egg yolks, beaten
¼ cup water
1 cup whipping cream
¼ cup sugar

Prepare and bake pie crust. Preheat oven to 325°F. Beat egg whites until soft peaks form. Gradually add ½ cup sugar, salt, cinnamon and vinegar; beat until stiff. Spread in pie shell. Bake at 325°F. for 15 to 18 minutes. Cool. Melt chocolate chips. Fold egg yolks and water into chocolate. Spread 3 tablespoons chocolate mixture on meringue. Whip cream; gradually whip in ¼ cup sugar. Spread ½ of whipped cream on pie. Fold remaining whipped cream into remaining chocolate mixture; spread on pie. Refrigerate at least 4 hours. Serve well chilled.

TIP: *Pie can be frozen.*

Frozen Amaretto Creams

8 Servings

1 (8-oz.) pkg. cream cheese, softened
½ cup sugar
¼ cup amaretto
1 cup whipping cream, whipped
  Fresh raspberries, strawberries and/or blueberries
  Fresh mint leaves

Blend cream cheese, sugar and amaretto; fold in whipping cream. Mound mixture by ½-cupful on cookie sheet lined with waxed paper. Using a spatula or spoon, shape mounds into shallow cups or tart shapes; freeze. To serve, place frozen cup on individual serving plate; top with mixture of berries. Garnish with mint.

Coffee Almond Cream

6 to 8 Servings

*The Cookery, Minneapolis,
Sara Monick and Mary Tuttle*

A creamy ending to a special meal.

3 egg whites
2 tablespoons instant expresso coffee powder
¼ teaspoon salt
¼ cup sugar
2 cups whipping cream
6 tablespoons sugar
1 tablespoon amaretto
½ cup finely chopped toasted almonds

TIP: *For a milder coffee flavor, reduce coffee to 1 tablespoon. Garnish with additional almonds.*

Combine egg whites with coffee and salt. Allow to stand for 10 minutes to dissolve coffee. Beat until soft peaks form. Gradually add ¼ cup sugar; beat until stiff and shiny. Whip cream with 6 tablespoons sugar and amaretto. Fold almonds into whipped cream mixture. Fold cream mixture into egg whites. Spoon into individual serving dishes. Freeze. Remove from freezer 10 minutes before serving.

Recipe Matrix

These menu plans are only a starting place for many season's celebrations. This matrix was designed to offer additional choices, providing thirty additional menus to allow flexible and creative combinations.

Each main course featured in the book has been paired with two new menu selections — one for hearty appetites, one for lighter dining — and includes appetizers, side dishes, and desserts. The new menus have been designed with complimentary tastes and textures, presentation appearance, and preparation technique in mind.

The new recipes have various yields depending on their original use — be sure to check this information carefully before you begin, and make appropriate adjustments according to the number you're planning to serve. Happy celebrating!

MAIN DISHES	APPETIZERS	SIDE DISHES	DESSERTS
Veal Chops with Sorrel Sauce	Fresh Mushroom Pâté	Zucchini and Red Pepper Saute	Chocolate Angel Strata Pie
	Vegetable Pizzas	Risotto Milanese	Strawberry Imperials
Dijon Sausage Soup/Cream of Spinach and Clam Soup	Hot Red Wine Punch / Crocked Cheese with Cognac	Fresh Greens with Viltoft Dressing	Macadamia Fudge Cake
	Feta Shrimp Triangles / Pesto Stuffed Mushrooms	Rafferty's Golden Cheese Popovers	Coffee Almond Cream
Cajun Seafood Stew	Rosemary's Punch / Harvest Popcorn	Pocket Cheese Bread	Interlachen's Pecan Torte
	Sausage Puffs	Endive, Cabbage, and Walnut Salad	Peanut Fudge Ice Cream Bars
Ham Braised in Madeira	Old Fashioned Egg Nog	Rice with Raisins and Pine Nuts	Persimmon Pudding with Brandy Whipped Cream Sauce
	Crocked Cheese with Cognac	Asparagus Timbales	
	Asparagus in Mini-Crepes	Sweet Potato and Pear Casserole / *Cranberry Nut Sauce	Cranberry Pecan Pie
Gingered Pork and Scallions	Crudites with Hot Mustard / Crispy Chicken Wings with Sesame Seeds	Rice with Raisins and Pine Nuts	Orange Alaska
	Brandy Slush / Bacon Wrapped Shrimp	Grapefruit-Avocado Salad with Poppy-seed Dressing	Lucky Lemon Surprise
Whole Grilled Salmon with Dill Sauce	White Sangria with Fresh Fruit	Superb Wild Rice	Strawberry Bavarian Pie
	Cucumber Soup	Snow Pea, Mushroom and Red Pepper Salad / Cheesy Onion Bread	Brownie Torte

*Recipe is not included in the book.

MAIN DISHES	APPETIZERS	SIDE DISHES	DESSERTS
Steering Committee Luncheon Shrimp Salad	Asparagus in Mini-Crepes	Apricot Bread *Fresh Fruit Salad	Creme de Menthe Bars
	Sausage and Leek Tarts Parmesan Mushrooms with Grapes	Honey Lemon Whole Wheat Rolls	Lemon Mousse with Fresh Raspberry Sauce
Butterflied Leg of Lamb with Minted Hollandaise	Cold Watermelon Soup	Sauteed Potato Casserole *Fresh Broccoli	Brandy Shake
	Grand Sparkling Punch Fresh Mushroom Pâté	Apricot and Avocado Rice	Chocolate Souffle with Creme de Cacao
Italian Herb Chicken	Vegetable Pizzas	Italian Salad Pronto's Rosemary Rolls	White Chocolate-Raspberry Tart
	Tomato and Chive Soup	Gustino's Pepperoni Bread	Grasshopper Torte
Baked Eggs with Muenster Cheese	Crabmeat Puffs	Grapefruit-Avocado Salad with Poppy Seed Dressing	Very Intense Brownies
	Avocado Supreme	Blueberry Orange Bread with Grand Marnier Spread	Raspberry Mousse Meringue Pie
Garlic Pepper Steak	Green Gazpacho	Wild Rice Casserole	Chocolate Chip Cheesecake
	Pesto French Bread Slices	Italian Sage Potatoes Herb Broiled Totamatoes	Chocolate Crepes with Butter Rum Sauce
Grilled Walleye with Vera Cruz Topping	Hot Mustard with Crudites	North Country Potato Salad	Raspberry Cream Torte
	Brandy Slush	Parmesan Cheese Bread	Fruit Tart Valerian
	Bacon Wrapped Shrimp	Snow Pea, Mushroom and Red Pepper Salad	
Warm Shrimp Flan with Reisling Sauce	Mexican Cream Cheese Spread	Mediterranean Vegetable Pie	Mixed Nut Bars
	Baked Havarti	Artichoke Hearts with Fresh Mint	Rhubarb Strawberry Crumble
		Honey Lemon Whole Wheat Rolls	
		Salad Elaine	
*Turkey with Homemade Stuffing	Wild Rice Soup	Squash Puree with Sherry	Apple Almond Tart
	Holiday Cider Toddy	Zucchini and Red Pepper Saute	Praline Pumpkin Pie
	Harvest Popcorn Cinnamon-Glazed Pecans	Bulgur-Nut Pilaf	
Veal with Pistachios	Avocado Supreme	Festive Romaine Salad *Croissants	Brandied Apricot Sauce with Ice Cream
	Bleu-Cheese Stuffed Shrimp	Swedish Potatoes *Parsley Buttered Carrots	The Chocolate Roll Murphy Coffee
North Shore Chicken Salad	White Sangria with Fresh Fruit	Strawberry Bread with Strawberry Butter	Heavenly Blueberry Pie
	Fresh Mushroom Pâté	Parmesan Cheese Bread	Chocolate Crepes with Butter Rum Sauce

*Recipe is not included in the book.

Restaurants & Caterers

Atrium Cafe International
and Primavera
275 Market St.
Minneapolis
339-8322

Arboretum Tea Room
3675 Arboretum Dr.
Chanhassen
443-2460

Byerly's
3777 Park Center Blvd.
St. Louis Park
929-2100

Dayton's Marketplace
700 Nicollet Mall
Minneapolis
375-2761

Duggan's Bar & Grill
5916 Excelsior Blvd.
St. Louis Park
922-6025

Figlio A Restaurant
& Bar
3001 Hennepin Ave.
Minneapolis
822-1688

Fitzgerald's
175 E. 5th St.
St. Paul
297-6787

The 510 Restaurant
510 Groveland
Minneapolis
874-6440

Gallery 8
Walker Art Center
725 Vineland Pl.
Minneapolis
374-3701

Haskell's International
Wine Room
600 1st Avenue North
Minneapolis
333-2434

Hotel Luxeford
Cafe Luxeford
1101 LaSalle Ave.
Minneapolis
332-6800

Hotel Sofitel
Chéz Colette, Le Cafe
Royal & La Terrasse
5601 W. 78th St.
Bloomington
835-0126

Interlachen County Club
Edina

Leeann Chin Chinese
Cuisine
900 2nd Ave. South -
International Ctr.
Minneapolis
338-8488
214 E. 4th St. - Union
Depot
St. Paul
224-8814
1517 S. Plymouth Rd.
Minnetonka
545-3600

Lightly Epicurean
Kathleen Lightly
400 Hwy. 7
Excelsior
474-8336

Lucia's
1432 W. 31st St.
Minneapolis
825-1572

Lunds
1450 W. Lake St.
Minneapolis
825-4433

Minneapolis Marriott -
City Center
Gustino's, Fifth Season
30 S. 7th St.
Minneapolis
349-4024

Minnetonka Mist
4050 Shoreline Dr.
Spring Park
471-8471

Sara Monick, The
Cookery
4215 Poplar Dr.
Minneapolis
374-2444

Muffuletta In the Park
2260 Como Ave.
St. Paul
644-9116

Murrays
26 South 6th St.
Minneapolis
339-0909

Nigel's Restaurant
15 South 12th St.
Minneapolis
338-2235

Orion Room
IDS Tower
Minneapolis
349-6250

Pronto Ristorante
1300 Nicollet Ave.
Minneapolis
333-4414

Radisson South Hotel
and Plaza Tower
Shipside, The Tiffany
7800 Normandale Blvd.
Bloomington
893-8443

Rosebud Grocery
3600 W. 70th St.
Edina
926-1623
1605 S. Plymouth Rd.
Minnetonka
545-6514

St. James Hotel
406 Main
Redwing
227-1800

The Saint Paul Hotel
L'Etoile, The Cafe
350 Market St.
St. Paul
292-9292

The Studio Restaurant
The Minneapolis Society
of Fine Arts
2400 3rd Ave. South
Minneapolis
870-3180

Mary Tuttle
The Cookery
7030 Willow Creek Rd.
Eden Prairie
941-8427

We Cater To You
Julie and Duane Wade
1039 Winnetka Ave.
Golden Valley
546-4287

Contributors

Barbara Aamoth
Stacy Allen
*Betsy Allen
Ann Althauser
Anne Anderson
Elizabeth Hood Anderson
Judith Anderson
Julie Anderson
Lynn Anderson
Amy Asta
Barbara Bachman
Pamela Badger
Sharon Baird
Sue Bakke
*Pat Bastian
Donna Beck
Laura Bedwell
Deborah Berg
Mary Bergaas
*Ann Besinger
*Cindy Beukema
Marilou Birkeland
Ann Birt
*Susan Bisanz
Laurie Blair
Jackie Bloom
Geraldine Bloomer
Patricia Bolin
*Terry Bolin
*Joyce Bowlsby
Katherine Bradbury
Anne Braun
Katherine Bredesen
*Ann Brilley
Susan Bruesehoff
Rebecca Bruggs
Theresa Bundick
Susan Burke
Mary Butler
Cynthia Cairney
Mary Carlsen
Barbara Carlson
Marsha Carlson
Patricia Carmody
*Sandy Casmey
*Marjorie Champlin
Elayne Chiat
Jennifer Clark
*Dru Clark
*Nancy Clemens
Mary Ann Clifford
*Diane Clift
Mary Frances Coffey
Nancy Cole
Deborah Cole
*Barb Cole
*Deborah Coleman
Margaret Collier
Phyllis Colwell
Meg Connolly
Virginia Cothran
Page Cowles
Lucia Crane
*Carol Cronk
Kathleen Culhane
Kathleen Currie
Kathy Daugherty

Julie Daugherty
Monica Day
Sandy Day
*Shirley Dayton
*Bette DeMars
*Mimi Dennehy
Margaret Dickhaus
Donna DiPadua
Nancy Donnelly
Julie Drake
Patricia Duggan
Denise Durante
Christine Earls
*Judy Ebrahim
Lisa Eckert
Michelle Eisele
Kathy Eller
Mary K. Ellingen
Patricia Engel
Elizabeth Erickson
Joy Erickson
Sandra Esmay
*Camie Eugster
Kathleen Feely
Jane Fellows
*Joan Fink
*Barbara Fischer
Rosemary Fish
Therese Fitzgibbons
Sally Fletcher
Carol Foster
Kathy Fox
Margene Fox
*Ellen Frank
Kay Franzen
*Mary Freeman
Karlynn Fronek
Jan Fugler
Christine Gabrielson
Jenny Garthwaite
Kathryn Gilbertson
Patricia Gilligan
Ann Goodfellow
Jenny Goodman
Jane Gordon
Penelope Grabek
Zylpha Gregerson
*Jane Gregerson
*Sue Ann Gruver
*Barbara Gullickson
Susan Gullickson
Sue Gulliford
Judy Hagglund
Julie Hahn
Barbara Halbakken
*Julia Hallquist
*Carol Hancock
Katherine Harder
Joan Harris
Elizabeth Hartman
*Kristina Hatch
*Bonnie Hayden
Diane Heacox
Linda Helmstetter
Linda Hendrickson
Gretchen Hendrikson
Patricia Hershock

Marlys Herstad
*Linda Higgins
*Sue Hodder
Mary Hodgdon
Joan Hoffman
Sally Hofmeister
Happy Hoofers
*Linda Hopkins
Claire Horner
Mary Howard
Stacy Hudgens
Jan Humphrey
Kathleen Humphries
Mary Ingebrand-Pohlad
Margaret Jennings
Lynda Johnson
Ann Johnson
*Susan Johnson
Nancy Jones
Susan Jorgensen
*Ann Jung
Cynthia Jurgenson
Cynthia Kaiser
Mary Karinen
Stefanie Karon
*Patricia Kennedy
Suzanne Knelman
Patricia Kopriva
Carol Korda
*Pam Korell
*Coralyn Koschinska
Judy Kramer
*Mary Kunz
*Amy Campbell Lamphere
Katherine Lang
Lucy Larson
Deborah Laub
Nancy Lazenga
Ruth Lazzeroni
Sydney Leathers
Joan Lewis
Florice Lietzke
Dorothy Liljergren
Mary Lilly
Nancy Lindahl
*Sara Lindahl
Nancy Lindley
Harriet Ludwick
Kathy Magers
Wendy Maguire
Jan Manning
Deborah Margeson
Carol Martin
Dianne May
Marcia Mayo
*Barbara McCabe
Mary McCary
Karin McCoy
Sue McDonald
Nancy McGoldrick
*Ellie Meade
Claire Meister
*Velia Melrose
Barbara Melsen
*Judy Mendesh
Janis Gail Merrill
Susan Merriman

Kimberley Meyer
Cherie Middleton
Joan Miesbauer
Jacque Mihm
*Karen Miller
Susan Mitchell
Sara Monick
Barbara Monroe
Anne Monteith
Barbara Moore
*Nicole Moore
Kay Moos
Susan Morken
Joan Mowatt
*Ellen Mueller
Patricia Murphy
Colleen Murphy
Janet Neff
Nancy Nelson
Janet Nelson
*Judy Neumeier
Deirdre Newell
Judy Norback
Karen Norman
*Mary Norris
*Mary Nusser
Carolyn Olson
*Sylvia Olson
Barbara Ostapina
Marcia Otte
Edan Paar
Marilyn Palmby
Lesya Parekh
Nancy Parker
*Penny Paulson
*Jill Peacock
Brenda Pearson
*Marcia Pertuz
Gail Peterson
Margaret Peterson
Dianne Petrzelka
Betty Peyton
Vicky Pierce
Mary Kay Pilla
*Kathy Pluhar
Molly Poole
Wendy Powell
*Nancy Priedemann
Patricia Priesmeyer
Nathalie Pyle
Pat Quinlan
Robin Rasmussen
Katherine Recher
Alice Reimann
*Mary Revello
*Stella Rezac
Tracee Rich
Joan Rischall
Mary Robbins
*Helen Rockwell
*Ann Ryan
*Colleen Ryan
Karen Rye
Jane Sangalis
Theodora Santrizos
Pamela Saunders
Jo Ellen Saylor

*Lynn Schaefer
Margy Schaller
*Lisa Schaller
Catherine Schmoker
Gail Schmoller
*Marian Schrah
Mary Schrock
Barbara Schulz
Claudia Sefton
Denis Shackleton
Barbara Sill
Connie Simons
*Patricia Sinclair
Lisa Skoog
Cynthia Sorensen
Cynthia L. Sorenson
*Linda Speece
Patricia Spencer
Margaret Spiegel
Arlys Stadum
Ruth Stevens
Jennifer Stoltenberg
*Kristine Strandness
*Kris Strawbridge
Susan Strobl
Jo Ann Stromberg
*Candace Struse
*Kathleen Suddendorf
Lynn Talbert
*Nancy Tarbox
Patricia Tarzian
Abbie Thiss
Martha Thomas
Kimberlee Thompson
Nancy Thomson
Nancy Thorp
Rita Thysell
Nancy Thysell-Johnson
*Debbie Tonissen
Judy Tucker
Mary Tuttle
*Nancy Tyra-Lukens
Pamela Ulvestad
Mary Kay Underwood
Kathy Urseth
Mary Catherine Van Der Naillen
Linda Vogel
Julie Waycoff
*Barbara Weikart
Karen Werner
*Mary Kathryn Werner
Robin Westin-Schmit
Pamela Weston
Cynthia Whisnant
Virginia White
Barbara Wilk
*Jane Wine
*Martha Winum
Jean Wohlrabe
Jane Wood
Nancy Wyatt
Mary Youngquist
Holly Yue
Mary Lange Zbikowski
*Bobo Zinn

*Denotes Recipe Tester

Acknowledgements

The artist, ELIZABETH HOOD ANDERSON grew up in Mahtomedi, Minnesota and is a graduate of the Minneapolis School of Art and Design. She has studied with such nationally known watercolorists as Edgar A. Whitney, Robert E. Wood, Charles Reid, Frank Webb and Zoltan Szabo.

After years of work in the advertising field, combining her interest in design and illustration with marriage and the raising of two children, she now devotes her time to painting and teaching workshops around the United States.

The recipient of numerous awards, Anderson has exhibited widely at universities and private institutions in the upper midwest and southeastern states. Her work is featured in private and corporate collections and in selected galleries across the United States and abroad.

CELEBRATED SEASONS was designed by MORGAN WILLIAMS & ASSOCIATES, INC., a ten-year-old graphic design company located in downtown Minneapolis.

Starr Morgan and Andrea Williams have developed innovative design concepts for numerous clients in the Twin Cities.

The wine selections for CELEBRATED SEASONS menus have been made by JOHN FARRELL, President of Haskell's International Wine Room, located in the heart of downtown Minneapolis. Haskell's is one of the largest importers of fine wines in the world, and has served the Minneapolis entertainment market since 1934. Farrell has been honored by numerous wine trade organizations and holds memberships in many wine societies in the United States and abroad.

Farrell has a daily radio show, "Entertaining Ideas," on CBS Radio. He is the publisher of a national wine newsletter and has been a contributing editor to many periodicals on the subject of wine and food.

The copy for CELEBRATED SEASONS was written by AMY CAMPBELL LAMPHERE, a member of the Junior League of Minneapolis and a food writer in the Twin Cities. She is a member of the International Association of Cooking Professionals and is an experienced caterer, restaurant consultant and teacher. She has worked with the Silver Palate in New York City as Director of Retail Promotions and assisted in the development of the Silver Palate Cookbook. Her restaurant, recipe and entertaining column, "Appetite," is a weekly feature in City Pages, the Weekly Newspaper of the Twin Cities.

Index